THE COUNTRY LIFE COOKERY BOOK

Persephone Book N° 109
Published by Persephone Books Ltd 2014

First published by
Country Life in 1937

© Country Life 2014

Preface © Simon Hopkinson

Endpapers taken from an early 1930s
design for a screen-printed textile by
Josef Hillerbrand for Morton Sundour
© V & A Images

Typeset in ITC Baskerville by
Keystroke, Wolverhampton

Colour by Banbury Litho

Printed and bound in Germany by
GGP Media GmbH, Poessneck

ISBN 978 1 903155 998

Persephone Books Ltd
59 Lamb's Conduit Street
London WC1N 3NB
020 7242 9292

www.persephonebooks.co.uk

THE COUNTRY LIFE COOKERY BOOK

by

AMBROSE HEATH

✳✳✳✳✳✳✳

with illustrations by

ERIC RAVILIOUS

and a new preface by

SIMON HOPKINSON

PERSEPHONE BOOKS
LONDON

PREFACE

✲✲✲✲✲✲✲✲

That which I find most appealing when reading *The Country Life Cookery Book* is how the resonance of each recipe is more sensibly, curiously, charmingly and quirkily English than most cookery writing since. Although there are plenty of references to what I still like to call 'continental' recipes in Ambrose Heath's unique collection, he handles the mood and period with a voice that is entirely that of a home-grown enthusiast. An intellect and ingenuity, thrift and humour, good taste and provenance, together with a charming indifference to a majority of precise measurements or timings, quite delight this present day reader. I would give anything to be allowed to compose recipes this way, this day, for a cookery book – and to have the beautiful engravings of Eric Ravilious as decoration throughout just as a wistful reverie. . .

Ambrose Heath was a highly respected journalist who worked on *The Manchester Guardian* and *The Times*, before a love of cookery writing became his preferred *œuvre*. As well as *The Country Life Cookery Book*, another admirable publication was his exact and enthralling translation of Madame Prunier's *Fish Cookery* (1938), a first edition of which I treasure, turning to it when an entire turbot, say, needs fettling. And, make no mistake, the author's knowledge and expertise are clearly evident in the French mode, with *le mode* with tripe as fashioned in Caen. This alone would have been thoroughly approved of by any French chef, if it were not also for an *echt* sauce béarnaise recipe that would have pleased the imperious Prunier herself. Both of these are to be found in the first chapter, January.

As you may have guessed, this is then followed by a remaining eleven months of seasonal recipes, as well as a 'kitchen garden' preface to each chapter. Seasonal is simply how it was. Those of my parents' generation, as well as that of Mr Heath, knew nothing else other than, say, the purchase of a pound of leeks from the greengrocer in winter, followed by no leeks at all, all summer long. And although I enjoy and respect the natural restrictions that our beloved Albion is blessed with, cultivation-wise, I do now enjoy the option of serving up an ice-cold bowl of vichyssoise on a sweltering July day made with an out of season allium.

Interestingly, Ambrose Heath's recipe for 'leeks à la Grecque' in the cold month of February has, possibly, one of the most authentic instructions for making this dish that I have ever read. He says that the dish is 'agreeable' (a description I favour; superlatives are not Heath's way) and 'it is essential that olive oil should be used and no other.' Much as one enjoys using good olive oils today, I often wish an instruction such as this could emphasise how it should be 'particular', rather than the ubiquitous lotion it has become today. But I will look forward to a warm dish of mid-winter leeks dressed

****

in sunny olive oil, preferably eaten while a blizzard rages out of doors. The author loves his eggs, too, of which there are many recipes both simple and involved. A dainty dish on toast with chopped eggs and anchovies ('Swedish Savoury'), for instance. Another of salt cod cooked with eggs. And, in April, some egg dishes from America. 'Buckingham eggs' is one of these (including an instruction to '. . . put [them] into a sharp oven' – a singular description that I will purloin), followed by 'Scrambled eggs (New York style)'. In May, we have 'Eggs Polignac'. His further indifference for the need to explain where these epithets (of which there are many in the book) originate may irritate some, but as they are so charming and curious, to force an explanation seems redundant. However, the *most* bizarre nomenclature of all (June) is one for 'Speldered Herrings'; there appears to be no such word in my dictionary.

Many of these affected dishes were a boon to those who serviced the kitchens and dining rooms of fine country houses in the 1930s. When planning menus and laying elaborate tables, to name the ingredients of a dish to a guest would have been seen as absurd and, more importantly, of no interest whatsoever. Something along the lines of 'Ah, Eggs Polignac, how lovely! Cook always does them so *well*, you know . . .' being more the pronouncement given. One must also remember that any cook employed below stairs in these inter-war years would have been seen as almost professional chef material today.

As a matter of course, it would have been inconceivable that a cook would not have known how to make proper sauces, fine stocks for soup, to skilfully braise and roast, make all manner of cakes, intricate pastry work and even pass off a very passable soufflé. Most of Heath's recipes may have been of *some* interest to such folk, but many would already have known how to prepare the majority, as well as having their personal interpretation, previously honed. Conversely, however, a housewife with ambition – and particularly one with time on her hands – might well have approached the recipes here with a similar verve her daughter would do forty years later when tackling a taxing little Robert Carrier number.

But here is an interesting question: how far have we advanced, culinary and literary wise, since Mr Heath compiled his delightful, seasonal cookery book 77 years ago? Seasonal cookery writing is all the rage, now, but this was not always so. Nobody worth their salt would now dream of giving a recipe for asparagus in November, yet it was seen as the height of sophistication to be served the same vegetable imported from California in smart London restaurants throughout the 1970s. There were *strawberries,* too! Now one can buy such things every single day from the supermarket as a habitual given, and thousands do. Be assured, if Ambrose Heath were alive today, I feel sure that he would find a way to 'spelder' both asparagus and strawberries. But possibly not at the same time, or for Christmas lunch.

Simon Hopkinson
London, 2014

THE COUNTRY LIFE COOKERY BOOK

CONTENTS

AUTHOR'S INTRODUCTION

EVEN when I was a child, forty years ago, the smaller country house had not yet been entirely divested of its domestic splendour. Food and service were cheap and there was a lavishness about country life which was very different from the present time. The intervening years have changed all that. To-day the country housewife is no longer at an advantage when compared with her counterpart in the towns and cities. As a result of the development of transport and cold storage, it is the same goods that she buys, only she finds it rather more difficult to buy them. She no longer makes her own bread and butter, and home-made butter is difficult to get and then inordinately expensive. Instead of half an hour spent shopping almost round the corner, and tradespeople delivering all day long, she has to motor to the nearest town, which means a morning's work, and then must bring her purchases home herself or leave them for the local carrier. And she will find that her choice is often severely limited, especially in those shops, such as the fishmonger, where perishable goods are only stocked regularly when there is a constant demand. Without some ingenuity, therefore, she may find that the scope of her culinary repertoire is somewhat circumscribed.

The domestic problem in the country is, of course, far more serious than it is in the towns. Houses that are some distance from a town, and often from a village, find the greatest difficulty in getting and keeping servants, who (possibly village girls themselves) find the life too quiet for them. Where forty years ago a servant would have gladly walked five miles into a village to meet a friend, she will not now cycle even two miles to see the pictures. Many country houses, too, can no longer afford the staff necessary to run the place as smoothly as in the old days, and consequently servants fight shy of going to a situation where they think they may have to work too hard. The country housewife, often in terror of losing her maids, has to think very carefully before she orders a meal, for fear of overburdening the kitchen staff. For in most country houses what I may perhaps call the Mrs. Beeton school of cooking still persists : an admirable school I agree, but often it demands more elaborate dishes than purse or personnel can manage. One of the purposes for which this book has been written is to give a selection of dishes which, while delicious and attractive in themselves, are quite simple and comparatively inexpensive to prepare. I have lived for the past four years in the country and I know from experience some of the difficulties I have written of, but these dishes are all of the kind that have been cooked in my own home, and by my own hands. I contend (I am sure rightly) that if I, who have many other duties to perform beside that of cooking, find that these dishes do not take up too large an amount of my time, a servant who is paid to do nothing else but cook cannot object to them on the score that they take too long to do.

Dishes which seem to the inexperienced to be really "party" dishes turn out to be of the kind that any cook can serve up for luncheon. I have confined myself to those ingredients which can readily be purchased in the ordinary country town, and I have kept my eye on ways of utilising the different sorts of game which may find their way into the larder by gun or by gift. A special chapter is added at the end about river fishes, often a stumbling-block to the uninitiated.

One other thing I have ventured to do. Mrs. Elizabeth Lucas, in her very attractive book on "Vegetable Cookery," offers the revolutionary theory that the gardener should be under the direction of the cook! The mistress at any rate can be the proper go-between, and in those houses where it is not already done I am sure that the mistress's intelligent supervision of the work of the kitchen garden would be a great asset to the table. We have all suffered from gardeners with a passion for size, and we have perhaps given way to them although we know in our hearts that it is the young things, whether vegetable or animal, that are the best. The gardener's overplus is something against which every cook and housewife should fight to the death. I have often wondered why gardeners always sow or plant at least twice as much as the household can possibly need. Whether it is just through horticultural wantonness or because he is afraid that if he does not plant much too much he will not have enough, I do not know. But much space is wasted by this ridiculous practice, and it has the result that we have to eat up his vegetables long after they are too old to eat, while we must complain that we haven't the room for some particularly choice novelty we should have liked to try. In the little introductions to each month of recipes, therefore, I have jotted down a few hints which will remind the housewife to remind the gardener of those duties which will later in the year have contributed so much to the delights of the table.

One last word. There are two things which have made my own kitchen-gardening particularly interesting. One is the growing of unusual vegetables, among which I would especially mention corn salad, celeriac, and custard marrows, about which, and others, I shall write in the months that follow. The other is the entrancing use I have made of Continuous Cloches. I am not a believer in food out of season, and I can never understand why so-called gourmets take the trouble to pay twenty-five or thirty shillings a pound for forced strawberries that have little or no flavour. But the results which you get from the use of these cloches can hardly be called a forced result, for although you get your vegetable or fruit a good time before its normal season, it has not lost its flavour through the gentle treatment these glasses give it. And it is a real treat to be able to pick fresh lettuces out of the garden all the year round, to have one's peas and beans and strawberries a few weeks before other people can get them (what a chance for the hostess to shine, too !), and to be able to ripen one's outdoor tomatoes in a rainy summer. Looking through my menu-book, I find that in 1935 we were eating peas on the 26th June, strawberries on the 13th June, French beans on the 1st July, and new potatoes on the 9th June. The next year peas came on the 25th May, and strawberries on the same day, while new potatoes were three days late. It is not within the scope of this book to write as much as I should like about this kind of cultivation, but I do recommend those who are interested to write to Chase Protected Cultivation Limited, at Chertsey, for details.

AMBROSE HEATH

Cowesfield Green,
  16th February, 1937.

P.S. I strongly advise readers who keep, or are moved to keep, a record of their gardening experiences to arm themselves with a copy of Country Life's enchanting "Gardener's Diary."

JANUARY

THE KITCHEN GARDEN IN
JANUARY

ALTHOUGH there is not a great deal for the housewife to think about in the kitchen garden this
month, it is pleasant to dwell on the thought that on
the next few months so much depends for the delights
that we are to enjoy for the rest of the year. For
instance, what will May be like without plenty of
Asparagus? Now is the time to see that the beds are
well manured, and those who live near the sea will
find seaweed the best of all. Its use certainly saves
the addition of salt to the beds and greatly improves

its flavour, I am told, though I do not remember consciously making the experiment of contrast.

When the weather is suitable (but how often it isn't !), there is plenty of work to be done in trenching and manuring for peas and beans, and the more that can be done just now goes so far to help during the busier months of the year. Seeds can be sown in a sheltered border, or under the Continuous Cloches—*Radishes, Onions, Spinach, Lettuce, Cabbage* and *Carrot*, to say nothing of that attractive and easy-growing little salad, *Corn Salad* which is also called *Lamb's Lettuce* and the French call *Mâche*. Attention should be given to the business of forcing *Seakale* and *Rhubarb* ; *Broad Beans* may be sown under glass for planting out later, and *Horseradish* planted out for making good winter root.

In the greenhouse *Cauliflower* may be sown, as well as *Leeks*, and a few *Lettuces* on gentle hotbeds will not come amiss later on. The *Tomato*-grower begins to think about his seeds, and I suggest one of the yellow varieties this year.

NOTES

JANUARY DISHES

TWO CHESTNUT SOUPS

One Cook three-quarters of a pound of chestnuts, and pass them through a sieve. Put this purée into a saucepan and add a good sprig of parsley, a small stick of celery, pepper, salt, and a pint and a half of white stock. Simmer for an hour and a half, then add up to three-quarters of a pint of milk, enough to make the soup the right consistence. Pass through a sieve again, heat up and, just before serving, add a little chopped parsley and a couple of tablespoonfuls or so of cream.

Two Roast some chestnuts, peel them, and cook them gently for a few minutes in a little butter. Then moisten them with stock to which you have added a glass of dry white wine, and let them simmer until they are soft. Pound them now in a mortar, rub them through a fine sieve, and mix with a thin purée of game. Serve with croûtons.

FLANDERS LEEK SOUP

Cut up a handful of prepared sorrel (or spinach) leaves, two handfuls of chervil, six medium-sized leeks (the white part only) and two lettuces or endives, according to the season. Cook these in enough salted water to make your soup, adding a nice piece of butter, pepper, a few leaves of savory or basil and half a dozen medium-sized potatoes cut in quarters. Cook for four or five hours on a low fire and serve the soup as it is, crushing the potatoes coarsely with a wooden spoon. It is quite one of the most delicious herb soups there are, and I very strongly recommend it.

CELERIAC SOUP

Chop up finely a pound of carefully pared celeriac, and blanch it in boiling water. Then drain it and cook it for a little in an ounce of butter. Add two medium-sized potatoes also finely chopped and after a few minutes a quart of white stock. Simmer until the vegetables are tender, pass through a very fine sieve and let the result reduce very slowly for half an hour. Add cream if you like, but certainly have fried croûtons of bread with it.

23

As its name betrays, it tastes somewhat like celery soup, but more, I think, like a mixture of artichoke and salsify.

CURRIED EGGS WITH LENTILS

Wash half a pound of lentils and soak them for an hour before you want them. Hard-boil half a dozen eggs, shell them, prick them all over with a fork, and roll them in slightly salted curry powder until they are lightly covered. Bring to the boil a couple of ounces of butter in a saucepan, and fry the eggs in it for about five minutes, turning them and seeing that they do not burn. Take them out, and fry in the same fat a small onion finely chopped and, when this is golden, add a tablespoonful of curry powder and another chopped onion, and fry all together until richly brown. Drain the lentils now, and add them to cook for another five minutes. Then moisten with a gill of warm water, put in the eggs, and let all simmer gently till the liquid is absorbed and the lentils done. Serve very hot, sprinkled with freshly-ground black pepper.

FROMAGE D'ŒUFS

Break eight eggs into a buttered low soufflé dish of a size just large enough to hold them rather crowdedly, and see that they are broken carefully, so that the yolks are intact. Then place the dish in the oven in a baking-tin of boiling water, and cook them for ten minutes. When cold, the cake of eggs should be turned out on to a dish, and coated with mayonnaise sauce flavoured with chopped *fines herbes*, that is parsley, chives, chervil, and tarragon. (All these you should have under your glasses.) You can colour your mayonnaise green, if you like, or even pink with tomato purée.

OMELETTE PARMENTIER

Cut some raw potatoes into tiny and even cubes of about an eighth of an inch sides, and fry them golden in clarified butter. Drain them very well, and mix them with the eggs of your omelette before it is cooked, adding, if you like, a little chopped parsley, though the croûtons alone are best. Then make your omelette in the usual way. You will find the contrast between the soft omelette and the crunchy potatoes very nice indeed.

BAKED COD

Cut some raw cod into pieces of a size for serving and dip these in milk, salted to the extent of a tablespoonful of salt to each cupful of milk. Then dip the pieces in finely-sieved white breadcrumbs. Put the pieces into a well-buttered shallow fireproof dish, and sprinkle them with melted butter. Bake quickly in a hot oven (about 550° F.), and they will be brown and done in ten minutes.

COD WITH HORSERADISH

It is uncommon to find horseradish used for much else than an accompaniment to roast beef, and it is such a weed that it is a pity we cannot make greater use of it. Here is one, however, which may be new.

Cook about two pounds of cod or hake, sliced or whole, in fish stock or water, and, when it is done, drain it and keep it warm. With two tablespoonfuls of butter, the same of flour and sufficient of the fish stock make a thick sauce. Flavour this with salt, pepper, and a tablespoonful of lemon juice, and finally add a couple of tablespoonfuls of grated horseradish. Do not cook after the horseradish has been added, and pour it all over the fish on serving.

SKATE A LA PROVENÇALE

Skate is a repulsive-looking fish if exhibited whole, but our fishmongers are mostly merciful, and sell it only in pieces. It is excellent if properly cooked, and a little more trouble should be taken over it than just boiling it in salted water. If you pour into the pan enough water to cover the fish by half an inch, and you add to this water, per pint and a half, half an ounce of salt, three tablespoonfuls of vinegar, three ounces of onion cut in rings, four or five parsley stalks, a sprig of thyme, and half a bayleaf, and then poach the fish gently in this, you will be rewarded. When the fish is cooked, put it into a shallow buttered fireproof dish, cover it with the flesh (no skin, pith or pips) of roughly chopped tomatoes, moisten with some of the cooking liquid flavoured with anchovy essence and lemon juice, and just simmer gently for fifteen minutes. Sprinkle over some chopped parsley, or better, *fines herbes*, before serving.

SOLE WITH SPINACH

Lemon, or Torbay, sole will do for this dish. Have the fish filleted, flour and season the fillets, and cook them in butter until golden on each side. Arrange them round a heap of cooked spinach with which you have mixed some finely minced onion fried separately in butter. Sprinkle some breadcrumbs over the dish, add a little melted butter, and brown quickly in the oven.

GOULASH OF BEEF

No household ought to be without paprika pepper, that deliciously fragrant pepper from Hungary. This dish needs it. Fry three pounds of beefsteak, cut in one-inch-sided cubes, in a quarter of a pound of lard with half a pound of coarsely chopped onions. When the latter are golden, add a teaspoonful of salt, a pound of peeled and quartered tomatoes, as much paprika as you like but not less than a teaspoonful, and a cupful of water. Cover, and cook in the oven for an hour and a half, then add a pound or so of smallish potatoes cut in quarters and another cup of water. Cook again, covered, for an hour or so, when the liquid will have practically disappeared. Serve as it is—and very good it is, too. It would be good for a shooting luncheon, if it is cold and frosty.

TOURNEDOS A LA BÉARNAISE

One of the simplest and yet most delicious meat dishes there are. The tournedos should be cut from the heart of the fillet of beef, and they are usually about an inch thick, not less, and two and a quarter inches in diameter. For this dish, they are grilled, and served on croûtons of fried bread cut to the same size and garnished with Château potatoes (that is, potatoes cut in the shape of a large olive, blanched, and then fried in butter until soft within and golden without). The Béarnaise sauce with which they are accompanied is made thus. Finely chop two shallots, and cook them with a glass of white wine and a dash of tarragon vinegar until the liquid is reduced by a third. Pour the strained liquid over three egg-yolks mixed with a small piece of butter and a spot of cayenne pepper. Strain again, and cook very gently in a double saucepan, being very careful that the sauce does not boil. When it thickens, stir in a very little lemon juice and some chopped parsley. (Chervil and tarragon are better than parsley, if you have them.)

A DISH OF LAMB

A very simple way of doing up some cold lamb is to make a sauce with a couple of tablespoonfuls of melted butter, three-quarters of a tablespoonful of vinegar, a quarter of a teaspoonful of mustard powder, and as much red currant jelly as your taste demands. Season with salt, pepper, and a little cayenne, and let the slices of cold lamb heat through in it, of course without boiling.

CUTLETS WITH GHERKINS

Prepare some rather lean mutton cutlets (best end of neck is the right cut), and fry them on each side in a little butter. When nicely browned, moisten with a few spoonfuls of stock and add chopped *fines herbes* (parsley, chives, chervil, and tarragon), a little minced shallot, salt, pepper, and a tiny pinch of spice. Let the cutlets cook in this a little longer, then arrange them on a dish, remove the grease from the sauce, add two or three gherkins cut in slices and a dash of vinegar, and pour this savoury sauce over the cutlets.

PORK CHOPS WITH GHERKINS

Have some pork chops cut as thin as possible, and fry them on both sides in butter or lard. When they are nearly done, throw in a handful of white breadcrumbs and, if you like the flavour (which really makes all the difference to this dish), a very little very finely chopped garlic. Fry with the chops until the breadcrumbs are browned, when the chops should be done, add then a cup of hot water (or better, of veal stock if you have some by you), and cook together for a few minutes more, so that the gravy thickens. At the last minute, having arranged the chops on a dish, add a drop of vinegar and some chopped gherkins to the gravy, give it a stir, and pour it over the chops. A really delicious dish, in which the gherkins lessen the richness of the pork.

FORT LINCOLN

This is an American dish, and useful for doing up cold pork. Cut three slices of fat pickled pork into cubes, and cook them in a frying-pan until all the fat has been exuded. Then take out the frizzled bits and all but two tablespoonfuls of the fat, and into the remaining fat stir three tablespoonfuls of flour. Gradually moisten with a breakfast-cup of milk to make a sauce, bring to the boil, season with salt and pepper, and simmer for a few minutes. Then add a breakfast-cupful and a half of cold cooked lean pork cut in small cubes, and send to the table within a wall of mashed potato. A grating of nutmeg in the sauce will do no harm.

TOURTE LORRAINE

Cut some raw pork and veal into thin strips, and let them lie for twenty-four hours in a marinade of onion, garlic, parsley, peppercorns, salt, cloves, and half a glass of dry white wine. Make some of your best pastry and line a dish with it. On this couch lay your drained and wiped strips of pork and veal, having removed all traces of the marinade, and put on the lid of the tart, leaving a hole in the top in which you stick a little funnel made of kitchen paper. Cook the tart for twenty to twenty-five minutes in a hot oven, and then take it out and pour in through the funnel two or three eggs beaten up with a cup of cream and slightly salted. Bake again for another ten minutes, and it is ready.

TRIPES A LA MODE DE CAEN

Here is a famous dish, for which so many ask for the recipe and which so few, I fancy, ever take the trouble to use. It is inserted here as being a possible dish for a shooting luncheon. Here is a recipe straight from Normandy.

Take two pounds of fine double tripe, scrape it and wash it well, and blanch it for half an hour. Drain it, dry it, and cut it into small squares. Cut also into squares the meat of one ox foot and one calf's foot. In the bottom of your large casserole put two or three pieces of the rind of pickled pork, the bones from the feet, two carrots and four onions cut in small pieces, a bouquet of parsley, thyme and bayleaf, tarragon, celery, a clove of garlic, four cloves, salt, a pinch of cayenne, and the pieces of tripe and meat from the feet. Moisten with a liqueur-glassful of Calvados (apple brandy), or brandy would do, and enough dry cider to cover the meat. Put on the lid of the pot, and seal it down with a paste of flour and water, so that it is airtight. Put it in a slow oven, and let the tripe cook for eight hours, " *à petits glouglous*," as my mentor picturesquely has it. On serving, the bones, the vegetables, and the bouquet should be withdrawn, and as much grease as possible removed.

COQ AU VIN

Not long ago a young friend of mine, enthusiastically returned from Corsica, asked me how to prepare the famous dish Coq au Vin, which he had enjoyed there. In case there are other returned travellers who may be of the same mind and come across this book, here is the recipe, practicable only for those who live in the country and can kill their chicken, as it were, outside the kitchen door.

Kill a fine young cockerel and save its blood, which you must mix with two small spoonfuls of brandy and half a tablespoonful of vinegar to prevent it from coagulating. Cut the bird in pieces as for a fricassée, and sprinkle them with salt, pepper, and spice, leaving them for two or three hours. An hour and a half before dinner-time, fry in butter

29

in a stewpan large enough to take the bird, some small
pieces of breast of pork, a few small cubes of bacon, and
a dozen small onions. When these are done, add the pieces
of the cockerel, and fry these golden, too. Pour away the
fat, add a liqueur-glassful of brandy, and set it alight.
Then moisten with a bottle of burgundy, and season with
salt, freshly ground black pepper, a pinch of sugar, a
bouquet of parsley, thyme, and bayleaf, and a crushed
clove of garlic. Simmer for an hour, and ten minutes before
serving take out the pieces of the bird and keep them warm
on a dish. Take out also the bouquet, and bind the sauce
with a tablespoonful of butter kneaded with flour and,
very slowly, the cockerel's blood, being sure to stir all the
time and to avoid bringing the sauce to the boil. Pour
this sauce over the pieces of chicken and garnish with
croûtons of bread fried in butter. As with *Civet de Lièvre*,
the binding with the blood is all-important.

KILMENY KAIL

An interesting Scots dish with rabbit. Cut the rabbit in
pieces and put them into a pan with a piece of pickled
pork. Just cover with water, bring to the boil, and, after
skimming well, add three heads of prepared kale. Bring
to the boil again, and cook for three hours. Season with
pepper, and with salt if you think it necessary.

BAKED ROLLS

A very simple and attractive way of using " left-overs "
and other things which is not often met with. Get some
French rolls, and cut off the tops. Scoop out the crumb
in the middle, and brush a little melted butter over the
inside. Let the rolls brown in the oven, and brown the
cut-off lid, too. As soon as they are done to the right
colour, fill them quickly with a hash of your left-overs, or
a white fricassée, or a creamy stew of, say, oysters, put
on the top, and serve at once.

A CHESTNUT GARNISH

Chestnuts go admirably with hare and other rich game,

but how often chestnut purée is wet and tasteless. For a change the cooked chestnuts might be served straight from a potato ricer, or they might be cooked in a casserole, thus.

First shell and peel them, then bake them in the casserole in the oven, covered, in just enough good chicken stock to cover them. When they are ready, the liquid can be reduced a trifle, seasoned, and bound with flour and butter.

POTATO GNOCCHI

Boil a pound of potatoes, and, when they are done, mash them well with three-quarters of an ounce of butter, a small egg and one egg-yolk, salt, pepper, nutmeg, and a sixth of a pound of flour. Roll this preparation with floured hands into balls about the size of walnuts, poach them in boiling salted water, drain them well, arrange them in a buttered fireproof dish, sprinkle them with grated cheese and melted butter, and brown them quickly in the oven.

HARICOT BEANS AND ONIONS

For this rather unusual dish use an earthenware casserole if possible. Soak the beans over-night, drain them, and boil them in salted water until they are done. While they are cooking, chop up coarsely two or three onions and fry them brown in a little butter or olive oil. Drain the beans, add them to the onions, and season them with pepper, a little grated nutmeg, and a dash of anchovy essence. Moisten with a little stock, and go on frying them until the stock has disappeared. Then squeeze a lemon over the beans, give them a stir, and serve at once, very hot.

FRENCH FRIED ONIONS

A pet waiter at a City restaurant in my youth always used to insist on bringing me what he called " French Fried " with my grill, and very good they were, much nicer than the often greasy and soggy mass that goes under the name of Fried Onions. White of egg is the secret. Cut the onions into thin rings, dip these in flour, then in beaten white of egg, then in flour again, and fry them in deep fat. You will soon discover the difference !

COCONUT CUSTARD PIE

Slightly beat four eggs, and add to them six tablespoonfuls of sugar, a large pinch of salt, and three cupfuls of milk. Mix in half a cupful of grated coconut, and use this mixture to fill a flan case or shallow plate lined with pastry. Sprinkle a little more coconut over it, and bake in the oven until done. A meringue mixture of beaten egg and sugar can be put on the pie after it is done, and then browned lightly, if you like, but in that case leave out the sprinkling of coconut.

KAISERSCHMARREN

This is a sort of glorified pancake. Make a batter with half a pint of milk, six ounces of flour, the yolks of three eggs, a little sugar, and a pinch of salt, and add to it an ounce of stoned and roughly chopped raisins, an ounce of ground almonds, and, lastly, the three egg-whites stiffly whisked. Heat two ounces of butter in a frying-pan, and fry this batter until golden brown on both sides. Then tear it up into small pieces with two forks, and serve it very hot, sprinkled with fine sugar.

BAKED APPLE PUDDING

Grease a Yorkshire pudding-tin well, and line it with a thin layer of suet crust. On this put a thick layer of peeled and chopped apples, and sprinkle these with lemon juice and sugar. Cover with another thin layer of the crust, spread the top with golden syrup, and sprinkle brown sugar over it. Bake until the top crust is brown and crisp, and eat with gratitude.

PINEAPPLE (OR ORANGE) PANCAKE

Beat up four egg-yolks with four tablespoonfuls of sugar until very light, then add a tablespoonful of pineapple (or orange) marmalade, four tablespoonfuls of flour, four of thick cream, and a grating of nutmeg. Whisk the whites stiffly, and fold them into the mixture. Melt a piece of butter in an omelette-pan, pour in the mixture, and fry on a slow fire until a light brown underneath. Turn it over on to a dish, sprinkle with fine sugar, and, if you like, pass it very quickly under a grill.

GNOCCHI ALLA ROMANA

A pleasant savoury luncheon dish that ought to be more popular. Bring a pint of milk to the boil and sprinkle in five ounces of semolina. Season with pepper, salt, and grated nutmeg, and cook slowly for twenty minutes, preferably in a double saucepan. Then thicken it with an egg-yolk, and spread it to cool in a layer half an inch thick. When it is cold, stamp it out into rounds of two inches diameter, arrange these in a buttered fireproof dish, sprinkle them with a mixture of grated Gruyère and Parmesan cheese (or Cheddar would do) and with melted butter, and brown them quickly in the oven.

FRIED CHEESE

A very simple, but quite exquisite little savoury. Get a box of Petit Gruyère cheeses (the sort wrapped in tin-foil), and, if they are thick ones, cut them in half lengthwise ; if thin ones, cut them across. Sprinkle them with a little cayenne pepper, and egg-and-breadcrumb them twice, preferably using white of egg and fine browned breadcrumbs. Then fry them in deep fat until golden and crisp, drain them very well, and serve them quickly. They should be very crisp outside, and nice and runny within.

FEBRUARY

THE KITCHEN GARDEN IN
FEBRUARY

RAIN may have prevented as much work being done last month as you had hoped, and time must be made up now when possible, for as far as rain is concerned February has a worse reputation than January ! More *Broad Beans* can be sown, and *French Beans* under cloches and in frames. *Brussels Sprouts* can also be sown in a warm place, and *Cabbages* in a frame. A sowing of *Corn Salad* can be made again, in case anything went amiss with last month's. When the seedlings begin to grow, thin them out to six inches apart, and pick the leaves when the time comes like spinach, leaving more to sprout up. This plant is an indefatigable grower. More *Lettuce* should be sown, and *Onions* in boxes for planting out, if you did not do this last month. *Parsnips, Savoys, Spinach,* and a little *Turnip* should also be sown, and do not forget that the end of February is the time to start your supplies of Parsley, which with the help of the cloches will stand you in stead all the year round.

If your soil is a dry one, and the weather is fine, early *Peas* may be sown; and if you have not been taught, as I was, that shallots should be planted on the shortest day and gathered on the longest, you should see to yours now. If you are one of those wise people who like to eat *Globe Artichokes* when they are young, you might try sowing some in a frame this month. Transplant them into the open in April or the beginning of May, and they should be good for eating in the early autumn. If you grow your own *Garlic*, plant it now.

When you are considering your *Tomatoes*, see if you can find room for some *Capsicums* and some *Egg Plants*, too. These are better known in cookery as *Sweet Peppers* and *Aubergines* respectively, and recipes for both are given for the months when they are in season, and very delicious they are. They are grown in much the same way as tomatoes, and require about the same amount of attention.

NOTES

FEBRUARY DISHES

A THICK SOUP

For a good substantial soup, cut up finely a good-sized carrot, two or three sticks of celery, and a couple of onions, and fry them in an ounce and a half of butter until they begin to colour. Stir in an ounce and a half of flour and let this cook with them and brown lightly. Now moisten with two quarts of stock, and stir until it boils. Add a couple of ounces of rice, and simmer until the vegetables are cooked. Then add some little balls of sausage-meat (which you have rolled in floured hands, about the size of marbles), and let them poach for a quarter of an hour.

BRUSSELS SPROUTS SOUP

There are still some sprouts in the garden, but they are getting a bit too blown for cooking by themselves except in a purée. So make this soup with them. Boil a pound and a half of them in salted water with a pinch of sugar until they are tender, and then drain them and rub them through a sieve. Put this purée into a saucepan, add three pints of good stock, bring to the boil, and simmer for a few minutes, skimming if necessary. Season to taste with salt, pepper, and nutmeg, and at the last bind with a little cream.

EGGS SUR LE PLAT

(1) *Bressane.* Cover the bottom of a shallow fireproof dish, whether for one egg or for more, with tiny croûtons of bread fried in butter, and pour over them some boiling cream. Break the eggs quickly upon it, season them, pour more cream over the whites, and cover the whites with some grated Gruyère cheese cut in very thin slices. Put a little bit of butter on each yolk, and cook at once in a very hot oven until the whites are set.

(2) *Lyonnaise.* Chop up some onions as finely as possible, blanch them, drain them, and cook them slowly in butter without browning them. Now add some flour in the proportion of a teaspoonful for each onion, and, when it is well mixed, moisten with half stock, half milk, until you get a thick cream. Season this, and put half of it into

41

a lightly buttered shallow fireproof dish. On this lay as many nicely trimmed poached eggs as you want, close together, and cover them with the rest of the onion. Now sprinkle with finely grated Gruyère cheese, pour over a little melted butter, and brown as quickly as possible. The eggs should not be too well poached in the first instance, so that the yolks may still be soft when the cheese is browned.

EGGS A LA GRANVILLE

Hard-boil four eggs and chop them up coarsely. Then heat them up in a little brown onion sauce, adding finely chopped gherkins and a little grated lemon-rind. Serve hot, with fried bread croûtons if you wish.

EGGS A LA DREUX

For six eggs you will want four ounces of lean cooked ham or bacon, a dessertspoonful of chopped parsley, and half a gill of cream. Butter well half a dozen patty-pans each large enough to hold one egg, mix the ham, finely chopped, with the parsley, and sprinkle the inside of the pans with this mixture so that each is well lined with it. Now break an egg carefully into each, so that you do not disturb the lining too much, season with salt, pepper, and a touch of cayenne, and put a sixth of the cream on top. Dot each with a tiny piece of butter. Poach them in a pan of boiling water in the oven, and, when the whites are set, turn them out on to rounds of buttered toast.

BAKED HADDOCK

Baked fresh haddock is a good idea for those who do not confine themselves to salt cod on Ash Wednesday, but it too often makes an unnecessarily clumsy dish. Try next time removing the head, tail, and the bones, so that you have two large fillets, one from each side of the fish. Then bake these, tied together, with your stuffing between them. It is easier to serve, and to eat, too !

FISH PUDDING

Suet-lovers may like to be reminded (for I cannot hope to be the introducer) of a fish pudding instead of a meat pudding. For this you must make a filling of some such fish as cod, bound with a not too thick white sauce, and adorned with something like shrimps or mussels or oysters, to say nothing of a few mushrooms, the oysters for subtlety of flavour, and the shrimps (or prawns) for flavour and colour, too. Line your basin in the usual way with your suet paste, put in the filling you have chosen, and cook as you have always done before.

FRIED SCALLOPS

Fried scallops make a very delicious and unusual dish. The white part is simply cut in rounds about the size of a very large half-crown, then egg-and-breadcrumbed, and fried golden in clarified butter. I am told they may be fried in deep fat, too, but I think the slightly slower cooking in butter would be preferable. Some cooks like to soak them first in a little olive oil and lemon juice for half an hour, but if they are fresh and young there is no need for this extra trouble. The trimmings and the red part can be cooked up and served the next day in the shells *au gratin*.

FILETS DE SOLES MURAT

This is avowedly a party dish, but it is one of the most delicious dishes of sole that you can imagine. Have the fish filleted, and cut each fillet diagonally into small strips about half an inch wide. Dip these in milk, then in flour, and fry them golden in a little butter. Meanwhile have ready some little cubes of fried potatoes and some cubes of artichoke bottoms which have been tossed in butter. (These latter can be bought in tins, but they are rather expensive.) Mix these both with the pieces of sole, and pour over them some lightly browned butter flavoured with lemon juice. At the last moment sprinkle over some finely chopped parsley. See that it is very hot.

BARBUE HAVRAISE

My gastronomical map of France tells me that le Havre is the place for brill, and here is a local recipe for cooking this pleasant fish. Get a whole fish weighing two or three pounds, and, when it has been cleaned, make an incision right down the backbone on the black side of the fish. Then lay it, black side down, in a fireproof dish (in which it will be served), butter well with about an ounce of butter. Sprinkle the fish with salt, and dot it with another ounce of butter in small pieces. Do not add any liquid. Now cover the dish with another one, or a lid, or some buttered paper, and either put it in a very slow oven for twenty-five minutes or on the top of the stove—in a place slow enough to prevent the juices from the fish coming to the boil, for a good half-hour. Baste it every five minutes, and when you can easily pierce the thickest part with a skewer, it is done.

Meanwhile make a white *roux* with an ounce of butter and an ounce of flour, and moisten it with a gill of fresh thick cream, adding by spoonfuls, stirring all the time, and being careful to see that it does not reach boiling point. Then when all is mixed well together, throw in half a pound of freshly picked shrimps, and keep the sauce warm. A few minutes before serving drain off the liquor from the fish as completely as you can, and add it to the sauce. Season this, and pour it over the brill to serve.

CREOLE FISHCAKES

Flake up the remains of any white cooked fish with a finely chopped onion, parsley, thyme, and a touch of garlic, mix well together, adding a tablespoonful of butter and one-third of the volume of the mixture in breadcrumbs. Shape into cakes or balls, roll them in beaten egg and then in breadcrumbs, and fry in butter or deep fat until golden.

POTATO ROLL

Potato roll is a rather unusual savoury dish for luncheon. Make half a pound of pastry and roll it out thinly. Mash six ounces of boiled potato with three tablespoonfuls of butter, season with pepper, and add a couple of table-spoonfuls of grated cheese and the yolks of three eggs. Now add the stiffly whipped whites and spread the mixture on the pastry. Roll up, shape into a roll or a crescent, brush over with melted butter, and bake for half an hour in a moderate oven. A tomato sauce goes rather well with this uncommon dish.

PAPRIKA MEATS

Most people who have consciously tried Hungarian paprika pepper develop a strong liking for it. Here is a good way of using it, almost nicer than the Goulash recommended last month. Cut up into small pieces a quarter of a pound each of lean beef, veal, and fresh pork. Cut up a couple of onions, and fry them in two tablespoonfuls of lard. Then add a teaspoonful of paprika pepper, a little salt, and the pieces of meat. Put on the lid, and stew until the meat is tender, adding now and then a little water to keep the meat from burning. When the meat is done, add a pound of potatoes cut in very small cubes, cook on, and, when the potatoes are done, serve very hot.

PORK CROQUETTES

Get the butcher to mince you, in his sausage-machine, some raw pork, half fat half lean, or, at any rate, two-thirds lean and one-third fat. Mix this well with twice its volume of mashed potato, bind with beaten egg, and season with salt, pepper, nutmeg, and finely chopped parsley. Shape into round flat cakes, like fishcakes, flour them, and fry them fairly slowly in butter until they are golden and the meat is cooked. Serve with a Sauce Diable or Piquante, and if you are the proud possessor of some pickled peaches, you will find that they go excellently together.

BUBBLE AND SQUEAK

Just a hint here, which may not be known to you—as it was not to me until a short time ago. After you have fried your mixture of potatoes and greens, stir in and cook with them for a few minutes at the last a beaten egg. An enormous improvement !

FILLET OF BEEF SOUBISE

A fillet of beef often makes a very good dish for a small family instead of the larger sirloin, and the following fashion is not expensive, although a trifle elaborate, and would be delightful for a luncheon-party. Lard the fillet, and roast it in the usual manner. When it is done, set it on a long dish and garnish it with medium-sized onions which have been cooked in white stock and glazed at the last minute. The sauce to be handed with this joint is a thin *Soubise* flavoured with paprika pepper somewhat highly. For this, stew a pound of blanched onions, finely chopped, in butter until they are tender. Moisten with a quarter of a pint of thick Béchamel sauce, and season with salt and a pinch of castor sugar. Now add a teaspoonful or so of paprika pepper, and cook together very gently for half an hour. Rub through a fine sieve or tammy-cloth, and finish with a couple of tablespoonfuls of cream and an ounce of butter in small pieces.

LENTILS WITH TOMATOES

This is a pleasant Italian dish. Soak the lentils as usual (get the greyish, flattish ones, not the reddish kind), drain them well, and put them into a saucepan with a tablespoonful or two of olive oil, season them with salt and pepper, and add two finely minced onions. Fry gently for a little while without any coloration, then pour in enough water just to cover, and cook very slowly, stirring now and then and, when necessary, adding enough boiling water to keep the vegetables covered. Half an hour before you want to eat them, add three or four tablespoonfuls of tomato purée, and let this cook with them, keeping it stirred occasionally.

CELERIAC PURÉE

If you have been wise, you will still have some celeriac roots stored in the same way as carrots. A purée of this vegetable is admirable with grilled sausages, and with dishes of veal, pork, and mutton. Peel the celeriac raw, as you would a turnip, and cut it into rounds or quarters according to its size. Put these into a saucepan, and cover them well with cold salted water. Put on the lid, and boil until it is soft enough for a fork to penetrate it easily. It should take about three-quarters of an hour. Now drain it well and dry it, mash it up, and pass it through a sieve. Mix it with a third of its weight of freshly cooked potato, and finish with butter and milk as in an ordinary potato purée.

ARTICHOKES

Artichokes (Jerusalem) are so often dull and watery when boiled, and we cannot always have them cut in very thin slices and fried in deep fat like chip potatoes. This way is worth considering one day. Cut a pound of them, peeled, in quarters and shape each quarter the size and shape of a large elongated olive, seeing that the corners are smoothed. Put a piece of butter the size of an egg into a saucepan large enough to hold all the artichoke " olives " in it and let the butter melt, and cook the quarters in it for a few minutes. Then cover the pan, and cook them gently for half an hour to three-quarters. When serving, add another small piece of butter, and sprinkle them with freshly chopped parsley.

POTATO SALAD

When next you are making potato soup, let me suggest this charming and, as far as I know, novel potato salad. Take your pared potatoes and, using one of the little *noisette* potato scoops (that is, one which makes little potato balls about the size of a hazel-nut), cut out as many balls as you want. Put them into a saucepan, just cover them with cold water, salted, bring them to the boil quickly, and then cook them very slowly and carefully, testing them now and again for softness. When they are nearly, but not quite, done, pour away all the water and finish drying and cooking them at the same time on the side of the stove. Let them get cold, and dress them as a potato salad in the manner you like best. These little balls served hot are very delicious, too, for garnishing certain soups. The reason for suggesting potato soup is, of course, because you will have a great deal of debris after your scooping operations. You will not want to waste this, and potato soup of some sort (with leeks for preference) is the best solution.

POTATOES WITH CHEESE

This is the famous *Gratin Savoyard*. Chop up very finely some raw peeled potatoes and season them with salt, pepper, and grated nutmeg. Butter a shallow fireproof dish, put in a layer of potatoes, and cover it with a layer of grated Gruyère cheese. Then more potatoes and more cheese. Moisten with good stock, dot with butter, and put on the top of the stove until the stock boils. When it has boiled for ten minutes, put the dish in the oven and cook it until the top is golden and all the stock has disappeared. Floury potatoes are best for this dish, and at a pinch a mild Cheddar could be used. But Gruyère is, of course, the proper cheese to use, and gives it the authentic *savoyard* flavour.

SPINACH PANCAKES

These can, of course, be made with good tinned spinach if necessary. They make an excellent accompaniment to dishes of veal, beef, and ham. Shred and parboil some spinach, and finish cooking it, until it is dry, in a little butter. Season with pepper and salt, and a touch of nutmeg, and mix it with an equal amount of the kind of batter used for making Yorkshire pudding. Bake in little moulds, and serve as suggested. The appearance of the pancakes is improved if the spinach is sieved, but if it is finely chopped it will do.

LEEKS A LA GRECQUE

This is really a dish of hors d'œuvre, but it could be served as a sort of salad if preferred. The leeks should be smallish and all of the same size, and they should first be cooked gently in salted water until they are tender, but not at all broken. Then drain them and lay them in a shallow fireproof dish with a seasoning of salt, pepper, and saffron. Add a chopped shallot and the flesh of a tomato cut up small, a bouquet of parsley, thyme, and bayleaf, and enough olive oil to come level with the top of the leeks.

Bring to the boil and cook for three or four minutes only. Remove the bouquet at once, and let this agreeable dish get cold. It is essential that olive oil should be used and no other.

SWEET SCRAMBLED EGGS

Scrambled eggs are seldom served as a sweet, but try this way some day. Beat up four eggs and add a gill of milk and two tablespoonfuls of castor sugar, as well as the grated rind of half a lemon. Cook in the same way as ordinary buttered, and serve with hot jam or a fruit sauce.

APPLE TART

Make a flan case of your favourite pastry, boil some apples to a pulp, and take a pint of it. While it is still warm add three ounces of castor sugar, three ounces of butter, the juice of a lemon, and the juice of an orange. When this mixture is cold, stir in the yolks of half a dozen eggs, and bake this in your flan case.

MARMALADE TART

Make your flan case, or line a dish with the paste, and on it put a layer of marmalade, orange, pineapple or ginger. Now take three ounces of sugar, three ounces of butter, and four yolks and three whites of egg. Mix these well together, put the mixture on the marmalade, and bake for an hour. Then beat up the remaining white to a stiff froth, spread it on top of the tart, and put it in the oven for a few minutes to brown very lightly.

CRÊPES PANACHÉS

If Pancake Day does not come in February, this dish will do for next month. Cream two ounces of butter with two ounces of castor sugar, beat in two eggs, and stir in lightly two ounces of flour. Add half a pint of warmed milk and don't be upset if it appears to curdle slightly, because it should. Beat well, and leave covered for an hour. Then butter half a dozen small plates, divide the batter between them, and bake them quickly until the batter rises, and then more slowly for about ten minutes. Put one on your dish, and spread it with hot jam, and do the same to the other four, each with a different jam, leaving one for the top covering. Dust this over with fine sugar, and serve this luscious pile very hot. Choose your jams as you wish, but I suggest that guava jelly might be one of them.

SWEDISH SAVOURY

Hard-boil an egg or two, and chop them up finely. Mince an onion, not too large, and fry it golden in some butter. Add a chopped anchovy fillet, or a teaspoonful of anchovy essence, mix together, and then add the hard-boiled egg. Cook together for a few minutes, and pile up on your toasts. You want to try and get a mixture so that neither onion nor anchovy predominate. The whole thing has a most attractive and indefinable flavour.

BOILED CHEESE STRAWS

Work a tablespoonful of lard into a pound and a half of flour, season with a pinch of salt, and work in three beaten eggs. Add a little water, until the paste leaves the basin in a ball. Roll it out and cut it into thin straws, drop these into a saucepan of boiling water, and as they rise to the surface, take them out and drain them. Arrange them on a dish, and serve them very hot, sprinkled with two tablespoonfuls of grated cheese and crisp hot breadcrumbs.

MARCH

THE KITCHEN GARDEN IN
MARCH

THERE is so much that can be done in March, that little is likely to be forgotten—if there is time to do it. It is a month when procrastination can be fatal. Let us go through the alphabet again. If you like *Jerusalem Artichokes* plant them now, and take a little trouble over them ; which they will repay, for the large tubers will appeal to the cook who has to prepare them ! See that the *Asparagus* bed is kept well weeded : it is most important. Sow main-crop *Broad Beans*, and plant out seedlings. Autumn and winter *Broccoli* must be sown during the month, and *Cabbages* sown again, especially some *Red Cabbage*, more often pickled than not, but delicious when eaten hot, as is explained in a later page. *Celery* and *Celeriac* must be thought of, if you sow your own supplies, the latter making a very attractive and unusual vegetable. *Leeks* must be sown now, and attention turned to *Cos Lettuces* for those crisp summer salads that are so cool and sweet. Sow main-crop *Onions* and *Parsnips*, but wait a while yet for *Carrots*, unless you like to try a few early ones. More *Peas* may be sown, and, if you like, a few *Potatoes* in a shaded place for earlies, most people preferring to defer the planting of the main crop until next month. *Radishes*, for those who like them, may now be started, and a succession kept up throughout the summer. Make further sowings of *Spinach*, and let me recommend the vegetable called *New Zealand Spinach*, which is not really spinach but tastes and looks like it when cooked, and is much less trouble to the cook as it does not require so much preparation before cooking. Outdoor *Tomatoes* should be sown now in the greenhouse, and a careful look should be given over the *Herb Garden* to see that all is in order there, and some plants divided and others sown.

NOTES

MARCH DISHES

POTAGE BONNE FEMME

Chop up two ounces of onion, and fry them in butter for five minutes without browning them. Shred an ounce of lettuce leaves and two ounces of sorrel, and add them to the onion with half an ounce of chervil, a good pinch of salt, and a pinch of sugar. Stir them all together over a low heat, and then add half an ounce of flour. Cook slowly together again for five minutes, and then gradually pour in three-quarters of a pint of milk and water mixed in equal quantities. Bring gently to the boil, and simmer quietly for fifteen minutes. Bind with an egg-yolk, and finish with an ounce of butter in little pieces.

CURRIED FISH SOUP

Skin, bone, and cut into small pieces a pound of fresh haddock. Brown them in a couple of ounces of butter with a peeled apple cut in dice, a couple of onions, chopped, and a teaspoonful of mixed herbs. After ten minutes add a quart of hot fish stock or water, bring to the boil, and simmer for half an hour. Now mix half an ounce of curry powder and two ounces of flour with a little water, and stir these into the soup, bringing it to the boil again and simmering for another half-hour. Then rub it all through a sieve, re-heat, season with salt, pepper, and a little lemon juice, and serve, handing hot boiled rice separately.

FRIED EGGS

Fried eggs certainly sound rather dull and breakfast-like. I do not, however, mean the fried eggs as we know them, but what the French call *œufs frits*—our sort of fried eggs being known to them as *œufs à la poêle*. A French cookery book rather cleverly describes the *œufs frits* as eggs which are poached in hot fat instead of in hot water, the only difference being the golden colour and crisp texture of the outside, the consistence of the white and the yolk inside the golden casing being the same as in the ordinary poached egg.

As in the case of poached eggs, you must have eggs that are absolutely fresh for frying in this way. Only one egg is fried at a time (you can't just fling them casually into smoking fat and hope for the best!), and in an exact amount of fat, about a gill and a half. Oil is best for the frying, but clarified butter can be used if oil is disliked.

A very small omelette-pan or a little saucepan are the best utensils to use, for it is important to see that this small amount of oil is as deep as possible. And you have to be quick about it, for the egg will fry in less than a minute. Pour the oil into the pan and heat it until it just begins to smoke, and as soon as it does so, move the pan to a place on the stove where the same temperature can be sustained evenly, and if possible prop the pan up a little so that the oil is nice and deep. Break the egg into a cup, season the yolk only with pepper and salt, slip the egg from the cup quickly into the oil, dip a metal spoon into the oil, and then draw the white over the yolk, so that the latter is covered. Turn the egg quickly over in the oil, and leave it there for a second only. It will be crisp and golden. Take it out, lay it on a clean cloth to drain, and fry your other eggs in the same manner.

You can serve them in various ways : on grilled ham or bacon, and with a tomato sauce as well, if you like the American fashion ; or on croûtes of fried bread which has first been lightly coated with some sauce or other, or they can be arranged to accompany a purée of some sort, potato, mushroom, tomato, or served with a savoury pilaff of rice. Whatever you do with them, they make a very good and very uncommon luncheon dish.

SALT COD (GASCONY)

Salt cod, with parsnips and a blanket of white egg sauce, is usually too dull for words and perhaps rightly confined to Good Friday. But the two following dishes will make you want to eat salt cod all the year round !

Soak the cod and cut it in fillets. Dry these well, and fry them in half butter, half olive oil, in a pan containing chopped anchovies, capers, finely chopped chives and parsley, and plenty of freshly ground black pepper. When

58

done, put it on a dish, and sprinkle over some browned breadcrumbs.

SALT COD WITH EGGS

This dish, which must on no account be kept waiting, is quite one of the most delicious fish dishes, I think. Soak and boil the cod, flake it up, drain the flakes as well as possible, and keep them hot. Now melt a good piece of butter in a frying-pan, add six beaten eggs, and cook slowly as for scrambled eggs. While the eggs are solidifying, add the pieces of fish, some more butter, plenty of freshly ground black pepper, and the juice of half a lemon. Finish cooking all together, and serve as it is, very hot, with perhaps some triangular croûtons of fried bread.

SCALLOP TURNOVERS

Blanch the scallops for five minutes in boiling water, bringing them to the boil in it, drain them, and enclose each one or each half one, if they are large, in a turnover of nice short pastry, enclosing a little white sauce made from milk and their cooking liquor as well. Bake in the oven for ten minutes, and you have another good luncheon dish. There is no reason why the white sauce should not be made more flavoursome by the addition of onion and mushroom, too.

GREY MULLET

Sometimes in a country fishmonger's you may come across an unusual fish, as I did once in a Winchester shop where a two-pound grey mullet was discovered. A very pleasant fish, and if you make the same discovery at any time, I advise you to buy him. But don't be tempted to stuff and bake him, as I was advised to do—but didn't. Poach him in a *court-bouillon* with vinegar, and eat his slightly gamy flesh a little reminiscent of mackerel with plain melted butter, or perhaps *beurre noisette*, which is lightly browned butter, and a few capers. The *court-bouillon* is to my mind essential ; ordinary salted water would have left him rather dull and flavourless. So this is how the *court-bouillon* should be made.

COURT-BOUILLON WITH VINEGAR

Cut up two medium carrots and two onions, and stew them in a little butter for five minutes. Add a bouquet of parsley, thyme, and bayleaf. Pour in your water and for each pint add a tablespoonful of wine vinegar. Bring to the boil, and simmer for an hour, adding a few peppercorns, ten minutes before the stock is finished. Strain well, and let it get cold before using it.

SALMON A LA CONDORCET

There is a divergence of opinion as to whether salmon should be cooked in water only or in a *court-bouillon*. I am of the personal opinion that if salmon is to be served plainly boiled, and especially if it is to be served cold, the use of a vinegar *court-bouillon* is unnecessary and the fish is better flavoured if only salted water is used. But if the fish has to be served with garnishing, which may detract slightly from its flavour, as in the case of the present recipe, then the *court-bouillon* is to be preferred. It is a very simple " party " dish. Poach the salmon fillets (or, if it is easier, cutlets), and when they are done arrange them on a dish, and garnish each with slices of tomato and cucumber which have been stewed in butter. Then cover them with white wine (*vin blanc*) sauce, and sprinkle each with a very little very finely chopped fresh parsley.

JOHN DORY

Another strange fish which may still be found in the fishmonger's this month. Many people recommend cooking the fish whole, but it is a large and repulsive-looking creature, and I fancy it will be preferred to have it filleted. In that case the fishmonger will probably make two large fillets of each fish. I have found myself that the most pleasant way of cooking it (and it has a decidedly attractive flesh) is simply *à la meunière*, that is, to fry the fillets in a little butter, after first flouring them. They are then served with a little browned butter poured over them, to which have been added a good squeeze of lemon juice and some chopped parsley. But I also have a leaning towards using olive oil for frying the fillets, and if that is done and they are first floured, they would be well accompanied by a *Provençale Sauce*. This is simply made by heating a little olive oil in a small saucepan until it smokes, then throwing into it some roughly chopped tomatoes, skin and all, a spoonful of chopped parsley, a pinch of salt, a pinch of sugar, and a crushed clove of garlic. Put on the lid, and simmer gently for exactly twenty minutes, then use as it is or strained over the fish.

The most popular way in France with this fish, which they call Saint-Pierre, is *au gratin*, the true *au gratin* and not the false one which to most people means cheese. Melt some butter in a shallow fireproof dish, and lay the fillets on it, having dried and seasoned them well beforehand. Pour in a wine-glassful of dry white wine, sprinkle the fish over with chopped mushrooms, and bake in a moderate oven, basting frequently, for about half an hour. Fish stock could be used instead of the wine, but the dish will not be so good.

FISH BALLS

Another good dish with salt cod, this time from America. Soak the cod, and cut enough small pieces to fill a large breakfast-cup. Peel and cut up some potatoes in even-sized pieces, and measure out two of the same cupfuls of these. Now cook the fish and the potatoes together in boiling water, and, when the potatoes are nearly soft, drain thoroughly. Put back into the pan, and dry them over the fire, then mash up well (without lumps !), add half a tablespoonful of butter, a good seasoning of pepper, and a well-beaten egg. Beat all this up together for two minutes, then take in spoonfuls and drop into deep fat.

PRAWN PANCAKES

Get a tin or glass of prawns or shrimps and toss them in a little butter to heat them well through, then bind them with a little cream or a thick white sauce made with milk and fish stock. Season with pepper and salt, and add a few drops of onion juice or some finely chopped chives. Make some thin pancakes, unsweetened, stuff them with this mixture, roll them up, arrange them on a long dish, sprinkle them with a little cream, or butter, and grated cheese, and brown very quickly. (If the prawns are large ones, they had better be cut up first.)

BAKED COD'S ROE

Cook a pound and a half of fresh cod's roe in milk and water for half an hour, and while it is cooking chop up a dozen sauce oysters and a couple of anchovy fillets (or use a little anchovy essence). Make a forcemeat of this with four ounces of white breadcrumbs, an ounce of melted butter, two beaten eggs, salt, pepper, and nutmeg. Cut the roe in slices, spread each with some of the forcemeat, arrange them in a long buttered dish, dust over with flour, cover with dots of butter, and bake fairly gently in the oven until the top is browned. Serve tomato sauce with it, or just slices of lemon ; but don't forget to take the skin off the slices of roe before dishing them.

VEAL WITH OLIVES

Get a nice piece of veal and brown it all over in pork or bacon fat. Take it out, and put in the same dish a few small onions, a crushed clove of garlic (if you like it), and a tablespoonful of tomato purée. Add a few spoonfuls of water, put back the piece of veal, and let it cook very gently with the lid on for a couple of hours. After an hour and a quarter, add a handful of stoned olives. If you prefer it, add mushrooms, peeled and quartered, instead of the olives.

CUTLETS A LA REFORM

I believe I am right in saying that this particularly attractive dish was invented for the Reform Club in London. Having trimmed the cutlets (lamb or mutton) well, dip them in beaten egg and then roll them in a mixture of equal parts of fine white breadcrumbs and finely chopped lean ham. Fry them then on both sides in butter or olive oil, and when they are done dish them up in a circle, the centre of which is garnished with julienne strips of boiled carrot, lean ham or bacon, hard-boiled egg-whites, gherkins, and truffles, the whole covered with Poivrade sauce to which have been added a glass of port wine, half a glass of Harvey's sauce, a teaspoonful of anchovy essence, and two good tablespoonfuls of red currant jelly. These ingredients are boiled with the sauce for five minutes before it is used.

Wonders have been done with cutlets and a kind of imitation Reform dressing, so long as the sauce is rich and piquant enough, and the julienne strips are there—even if you have to sacrifice the truffle. Only don't then call the cutlets *à la Reform*, but only an apology for it !

CHICKEN WITH SAFFRON

I suppose everyone has tasted saffron at one time or another, perhaps in Cornish saffron buns. It is not a very pleasantly flavoured spice by itself, I think, but it becomes quite admirable when mixed with others, as in this dish of chicken.

Braise the chicken in a glass of white wine and the same of stock, a large onion stuck with three cloves, a few small onions, two or three quartered tomatoes, a bouquet of parsley, thyme, bayleaf, celery, and tarragon, and, if you like, a clove or two of garlic. (Celery salt and dried tarragon can be used at a pinch.) When the bird is done, keep it warm and strain the liquid in which it was cooked. Now melt a tablespoonful of lard in a pan and add a tablespoonful of chopped onion. Let this cook gently without colouring while you wash and drain some Carolina rice, then add it, and let it cook for a minute or two until it becomes opaque. Then pour in the liquid from the chicken and enough stock to make twice and a half the volume of the rice. (That is to say, if there is a breakfast-cupful of rice, there should be two and a half breakfast-cupfuls of liquid altogether.) Season with salt, pepper, a good pinch of saffron, and a suspicion of nutmeg, and, after bringing to the boil, cook, with the cover on, in the oven for twenty-five minutes, when the liquid should all be absorbed and the rice cooked. Put the chicken in a dish, and bring it to the table with the rice round it.

LAMB A LA SAINTE-MÉNÉHOULD

This fashion, from the eastern border of Champagne, is most famous in pig's trotters, but this way with lamb is excellent. Put two good rashers of fattish bacon in the bottom of a pan or casserole, and lay on them some breast of lamb. Cover it with dice of fat bacon, a couple of carrots cut in slices, four finely chopped onions, and a bouquet of two bayleaves and a little thyme. Moisten with a couple of good tablespoonfuls of stock, and put on the lid with a piece of buttered paper under it, and cook gently in the oven for three hours. Then take the breast out, bone it, season it with salt and pepper, sprinkle it with breadcrumbs, and put it in the hot part of the oven. When the breadcrumbs are golden, serve it with clear gravy.

BRAINS

Brains make an excellent dish, though for some reason many people shy at them. Calf's brains *au beurre noir* with noodles are, in my opinion, exceptionally agreeable for luncheon. But this dish, which disguises their nature slightly, may be preferred by the ultra-squeamish. First cook the brains, and then press them under a weight until they are quite cold. Then cut them into nice little 'cubes and soak them in a little sherry for an hour or so in a covered dish. Now make a white sauce, enriched with cream and with a few sliced mushrooms lightly fried in butter. Add a dash of cayenne to it, and put in the brains, well drained, and warm them up. Sprinkle with chopped parsley at the end.

LEEKS AND POTATOES

Cut some leeks in halves lengthwise, and then cut them in pieces about an inch and a half long. Cook them in boiling salted water for about a quarter of an hour, then drain them, and keep them warm while you make a sauce with butter, flour, and some stock. Stir this until it boils, when you must add the pieces of leek as well as some potatoes cut in large dice, and let them cook there for thirty to forty minutes. Before you serve them, season them nicely. A pleasant mixed dish to eat with lamb.

SEAKALE

There are a great many ways of serving seakale, and any of these sauces can be handed with it : half-glaze, cream, Hollandaise, Mousseline (which is only Hollandaise mixed with whipped cream), Italienne or Bordelaise. There may be a good word to say for Hollandaise with it, for after all it is little more than plain egg and butter ; but by far the best of all is butter just melted by itself. If you want something a little more substantial, the Flemish custom of eating asparagus may be transferred here. That is to serve with the melted butter, half a hard-boiled hot egg-yolk to each person who can then mash it up with the butter and make his own sauce. If this sauce is handed separately, the proportions are one ounce of butter to each half egg-yolk. It might be noted, too, that Maltese sauce, which is Hollandaise made with the addition of orange juice and a little grated orange rind, is just as good for seakale as it is for asparagus.

Seakale makes a delicious cold dish for suppers, too. In this case it is best dressed with a mayonnaise *à la Chantilly*, that is mayonnaise mixed and lightened with whipped cream.

ONION PURÉE

Cut the onions in thin slices, and fry them in butter without browning them. Then add flour, and let it colour and moisten with half stock and half dry white wine, or stock only. Season with salt, pepper, and a good pinch of mixed spice. Finish cooking the onions in this, and then mash them up well and pass them through a sieve. Bind at the last moment with a little potato flour, and add some of the gravy from the joint you are serving them with.

SWEET CORN FRITTERS

People have sometimes asked me how to make the sweet corn fritters which are usually served with the famous

American Chicken Maryland. Others have wondered what to do with a tin of sweet corn at all ! Here are two sorts of fritter, one for deep fat and the other for shallow. Drain the liquid from the corn, and chop it up as finely as you can. Mix with it four tablespoonfuls of thick white sauce, season it with salt and pepper, and bind with two beaten eggs. Drop in spoonfuls in smoking hot fat, and, when golden, drain and serve.

CORN OYSTERS

Put two breakfast-cupfuls of tinned corn into a saucepan, bring to the boil, and simmer for a quarter of an hour. Then add a teaspoonful and a half of salt, some pepper, a couple of tablespoonfuls of milk, three-quarters of a cupful of cracker crumbs, and a well-beaten egg. Mix well together and drop, a spoonful at a time, into a frying-pan containing a little hot bacon fat. When both sides are nicely browned, the " oysters " are ready.

BUTTERSCOTCH PUDDING

Mix three tablespoonfuls of cornflour with a little milk. Now bring the rest of the milk (it should come to three-quarters of a pint in all) to the boil in a double saucepan. Add slowly to this five and a half ounces of brown sugar which you have already melted, stirring well, and a tablespoonful of melted butter. When the sugar and milk are well mixed together, add the diluted cornflour and stir until the mixture gets thick. Then let it cook for twenty minutes. Add a good pinch of salt and a teaspoonful of vanilla essence, fold in two stiffly whipped egg-whites, and let the pudding get cold. It will be improved at the end by a sojourn in the refrigerator.

MOCK CRAB WITH CORN

This time a savoury dish with sweet corn. Make a sauce with four tablespoonfuls of butter, half a breakfast-cupful of flour mixed with a teaspoonful and a half of salt, a quarter of a teaspoonful of paprika pepper, three-quarters of a teaspoonful of dry mustard, and a breakfast-cupful and a half of boiled milk. When the sauce is ready, add a tin of corn, slightly chopped, a lightly-beaten egg, and three teaspoonfuls of Worcester sauce. Pour into a buttered shallow fireproof dish, sprinkle with breadcrumbs, and brown in the oven.

LENTEN TRIPE

This is by way of being a modest little joke of somebody's. Make a batter with three ounces of flour, two eggs, and half a pint of milk, season with salt and pepper, and cook your pancakes. As soon as they are done, roll them up, and cut them across in thinnish strips, piling these up in a dish. Pour over them a thick white sauce, sprinkle with grated cheese, and brown quickly in the oven. If you like, you can add a very little chopped blanched onion to the batter, and flavour the sauce with onion, too. But add cheese, and brown as before.

ROSE'S SAVOURY

A contribution from a friend's cook. Boil a medium-sized onion, or more, until quite tender but not broken. Cut it in half and take out the centre. Chop this finely, and mix it with grated cheese and tomato sauce to your heart's content, season with salt and pepper, and fill the onion halves with it. Put a small dab of butter on each onion half, and let them brown in the oven. Half an onion, or so, for each person, of course.

APRIL

THE KITCHEN GARDEN IN
APRIL

HOEING and weeding seem to be the principal occupations of April, and the gardener's year begins with a vengeance. *Asparagus* beds should be salted, and the last sowings of *Broad Beans* made. Keep a look-out for black fly, and don't forget to pinch out the bean tops when the right time comes. If this is done early enough, I am told you can have a pretty dish of greens from them, but I have never tasted it. A few *French Beans* can be sown out of doors, and certainly under the cloches, and at the end of the month *Beetroot* may be sown for those smallish roots which are so much prized in the kitchen. *Broccoli, Brussels Sprouts,* and *Cabbage* can be sown, as well as the main crop of *Carrots.* Those who like, and have the room to grow *Cardoons,* should sow them now, as well as an outdoor sowing of *Celery.* Other sowings are *Leeks, Lettuce, Parsley* (and other herbs such as *Basil, Chervil, Fennel*), *Peas, Salsify, Spinach* and *Spinach Beet, Turnip* and *Kale.* *Cauliflowers* must be planted out when the weather is favourable, and any *Onions* sown under glass earlier in the year. The planting of *Potatoes* should be completed, not forgetting, as a novelty, a small patch of *Congo Black Potatoes,* which make such an attractive salad. And, lastly, some *Vegetable Marrows* should now be sown in pots, and in particular some of the custard marrows, which when very young make such entrancing dishes.

NOTES

APRIL DISHES

PORK AND PEA SOUP

Soak half a pint of split peas in two quarts of water over-
night, and then cook them slowly for two hours in the same
water, salted. Pass through a fine sieve, and in this liquid
cook two prepared pig's trotters for an hour. Now add
four onions (or leeks) and some celery salt, two ounces of
butter, and cook again until the onions (or leeks) are done.
Serve as it is, if possible in the earthen casserole in which
the soup was cooked.

YOUNG CARROT SOUP

A charming spring-like soup for which you will want some
young carrots. Scrape a pound of them and put them with
two onions, a bayleaf, and a little salt into two and a half
pints of water. Boil and simmer for three or four hours,
then sieve the carrots only into another saucepan, and
strain the liquid over them. Cook for a little longer, season
with pepper, and then serve after binding with yolk of egg
or a little cream.

CRAB SOUP

Fish soups are always particularly nice, I think, possibly
because we encounter them so seldom. *Bisque de Homard*
is beyond the reach of many cooks, but this crab soup is
quite easy to make. Take the meat from two cooked crabs,
setting aside that from the two large claws. Boil six ounces
of rice in milk until it is soft, then rub it with the crab meat
through a fine sieve. When quite smooth dilute it with
some fish stock and season it with salt, pepper, and a touch
of anchovy essence. Heat well through without boiling,
add the meat from the claws at the last minute, and finish,
if you like, at the last minute with a yolk of egg or a spoonful or two of cream. It should be rather highly seasoned,
and served very hot.

EGGS BUCKINGHAM

The three next dishes are from America. For this one first
make some pieces of toast, and dip each of them in white
sauce. Arrange these on a dish and on each put some

scrambled egg, which must be rather underdone. Sprinkle this with grated cheddar cheese, and put into a sharp oven to melt the cheese and complete the cooking of the eggs.

SCRAMBLED EGGS (NEW YORK STYLE)

Have ready a thin slice of uncooked ham or gammon of bacon, and soak it in lukewarm water for half an hour. Then cut it up in narrow strips ; there should be about a breakfast-cupful. Melt a tablespoonful and a half of butter in a frying-pan and fry in it a couple of tablespoon-fuls of chopped onion and the strips of bacon. After five minutes, add four or five smallish mushrooms, peeled and sliced, and cook for another five minutes together. Mix well and use as a border to surround ordinary scrambled egg. Sprinkle over all a little chopped parsley.

FLUFFY EGG NEST

This is not only attractive to children and invalids ! Beat up the white of an egg with a whisk until it is stiff, adding a small pinch of salt. Arrange this on a piece of buttered toast, and make a hollow in the middle to receive the yolk. In this hollow first put half a teaspoonful of butter and then the yolk, and bake in a moderate oven until the yolk is set. It makes a change for breakfast.

SCOTCH EGGS

Not the ones with sausage-meat, but a recipe from the famous Meg Dods. Hard-boil the eggs, then shell them, and dip them in beaten egg and cover them with a mixture of grated ham, chopped anchovy fillet, breadcrumb, and mixed spice. Fry in deep fat, and serve with thick brown gravy handed separately.

CURRY OMELETTE

Have ready a little savoury rice, which you have cooked in stock and flavoured with a little fried onion and tomato. See that it is nice and hot while you make an omelette with your eggs into which you have first beaten a little curry powder. When the omelette is cooked, fold the savoury rice into it, and serve it quickly with curry sauce poured round it.

BAKED SOLE (OR LEMON SOLE)

Have the fish filleted (but have the trimmings sent, too ; you will then have fish stock for a fish soup or sauce), and poach the fillets in the oven, salted, peppered, and with a squeeze of lemon juice over them and covered with buttered paper, for about ten to fifteen minutes. Strain off the cooking liquor, and keep the fillets warm while with a little butter and flour you make a sauce with that liquor, enriching it with a yolk of egg beaten up in a little cream. Pour this over the fillets, and either serve them as they are or garnish them with little olive-shaped pieces of cucumber stewed in butter or strips of tinned pimentos warmed through in butter.

PILAFF OF SOLE (OR LEMON SOLE)

This is a little more substantial than the above, but first cook the fillets in the same way as above. You will first of all have made some pilaff rice by cooking, covered in the oven, a cupful and a half of rice and three cupfuls of white stock, flavouring it with onions. Use this as a bed for the fillets, adding to it, if you like, some shrimps or pieces of prawns, or mushrooms, or perhaps some bottled mussels (which are excellent in a garnish like this). Put the fillets in the middle of the rice, and cover them with a Béchamel sauce, flavoured, if you wish, with a little cheese, but not too much.

HADDOCK PANCAKES

Often there is smoked haddock left over from breakfast the day before, and here is an amusing way of using it up, as a change from kedgeree. Flake the fish up fairly finely and mix it with an equal quantity of thickish white sauce made without salt, but with the addition of a little cayenne pepper. Make some thin unsweetened pancakes, and cut them into oblongs about two inches by four. On half of these oblongs put a tablespoonful of the cold fish mixture, and cover them with the other oblongs, brushing the edges with beaten egg and pressing them well together. Now egg-and-breadcrumb them, and fry them in deep fat. Fried parsley seems to be called for here.

DUBLIN BAY PRAWNS

These make excellent dishes. The simplest way of all is simply to shell them and serve them with a lettuce salad, just sprinkling them with pepper and lemon juice. Fried, they can be very delicious, too. Either dip them in milk and then in flour, or egg-and-breadcrumb them, and fry them quickly in deep fat, and they will make quite a passable substitute for the *scampi* which are so popular in a certain London hotel where they are brought over from Venice by air, I believe. But they will also make rather a good savoury luncheon dish, if, after you have shelled them, you sprinkle them with lemon juice and finely chopped *fines herbes* (parsley, chives, chervil, and tarragon), roll each in a thin rasher of streaky bacon, and bake them for about seven minutes in a hot oven. They are then served on buttered toast. But whatever you do with them, don't forget to use the shells and little claws for making stock.

SALMON BONE

The following suggestion is rather a greedy one, I fear, because it cannot often be indulged in by more than one person. But I do counsel the master of the house, or who-ever it is who next carves a piece of salmon, to see that a certain amount of flesh is left adhering to the bone. For this, when seasoned with salt and pepper, plentifully buttered, and grilled, makes a really delicious breakfast !

OXTAIL

Here is a substantial dish of oxtail which may be found useful on many occasions and is certainly a change from the usual " braise." Cut up the tail as usual, and put it into a stewpan with a pig's ear and two pig's trotters, each cut into four or five pieces. Cover with cold water, adding a third of an ounce of salt for each quart, bring to the boil, skim well, and cook gently for a couple of hours. Now add a small cabbage cut in quarters and previously par-boiled, ten little onions, and five ounces each of carrots and turnips which have been cut in the shape of olives.

Cook for another two hours, and then serve the tail with the vegetable garnish, the ear cut in thin strips and some grilled chipolata sausages. You will want no more than plain boiled potatoes with it.

OSSO BUCO

This very savoury dish made from knuckle of veal is a favourite Italian one. It is greatly improved by the use of a glass of white wine, though this can be omitted. Have three pounds of knuckle of veal sawn into two-inch lengths. Chop up an onion, a carrot, and a stick or two of celery (or use celery salt in seasoning), and brown them in a stew-pan in a little butter. Add the pieces of veal, and brown these too. Add an ounce of butter kneaded with an equal amount of flour, and let this brown with it. Now add half a pint of tomato pulp (or some tinned tomato purée diluted with water to make half a pint), a glass of dry white wine, and just enough water barely to cover the meat. Complete with a bouquet of parsley, thyme, and bayleaf (and add, if possible, a little basil), bring to the boil, put on the lid, and simmer for about an hour and a half. Strain the sauce on serving, and add to it at the last moment a little strip of lemon peel chopped up very finely with a few sprigs of parsley.

SAUSAGES WITH CARROTS

A little drop of white wine is also needed here, but it is so little that it cannot be called an extravagance, and after a dinner or luncheon-party there must be a glass or two left over for the next day's cooking ! Cook some baby carrots in butter and cut them in slices. Put them into a shallow fireproof dish and on them arrange some grilled thin sausages (the size called Parisian is the best for this dish). Sprinkle these with a little chopped parsley, some chopped fried onions, a drop or two of lemon juice, some of the fat from the sausages, and a glass of dry white wine, and cook together in the oven for just a few minutes longer. Serve as it is, with mashed potato.

PORTFOLIO HASH

Really an excellent way of using up any cold meat, particularly pork. Cook some *lyonnaise* potatoes. That is to say, first fry some chopped onion in a pan, put it aside, and, in the same pan, fry slices of cooked potato. Mix these, and cook them together for a minute, then put a layer in a shallow fireproof dish. On this layer put another of your cold meat chopped up or minced and bound with a sauce slightly diluted with stock. The sauce especially recommended is Escoffier's Sauce Robert, but his Derby Sauce and Sauce Diable would do very well, and even the cheaper and more popular sauces might be used. Then put another layer of the potatoes, another of meat, and a final one of the potatoes, sprinkling this with breadcrumbs. Sprinkle over a little melted butter, and brown quickly in the oven.

STUFFED LAMB

This is a cold dish, and so the lamb should not be cut until it has got quite cold. Bone a shoulder of lamb and stuff it with the following mixture. Fry lightly in butter half a pound of minced onions and three or four large chopped mushrooms. Add a small spoonful of flour and moisten with a cupful of milk. Season with salt and pepper, and, if you like, a touch of nutmeg, and let this mixture boil for a minute or two ; then let it get cold. Having stuffed the shoulder with this, brown it in fat or butter in a pan large enough to hold it, season again slightly, put on the lid, and cook in a moderate oven for an hour and a half. Let the shoulder get cold, and do not cut it until then.

TURNIP CROQUETTES

Turnips are always pleasant with lamb, but there are not a great many ways of serving them. As a change from the inevitable mashed turnip, let us try the following. Boil them in the usual way, then mash them, and dry them well over the fire, finally squeezing them even drier in a cloth. Now mix this purée with salt, pepper, and two egg-yolks, and when it is cold, shape into little croquettes, egg-and-breadcrumb them, and fry them in deep fat.

CAULIFLOWER A LA MILANAISE

This is a finer dish, I think, than the more popular Cauliflower *au gratin*. Cook and drain the cauliflower. (You will find here, by the way, that the French method of cooking a cauliflower is much to be preferred. They first divide the vegetable into its flowerets and cook these in boiling salted water. The advantage of this is principally that they all cook at the same time, whereas if the cauliflower is cooked whole, the flowerets are often overdone by the time the stalky parts are cooked. If you want the cauliflower to assume something of its old appearance, you can build up the flowerets in a pudding-basin after they are cooked, and carefully turn them out in a nice mound when dishing up.) When the flowerets have been cooked and very well drained, put them into a buttered fireproof dish which has been sprinkled with a little grated cheese, Parmesan in this case being the best. Sprinkle some more cheese over the cauliflower, add a little melted butter, and brown it quickly in the oven. On serving, pour over some *noisette* butter ; that is, butter which has been lightly browned until it begins to smell—and look—nutty. Some very fresh and freshly chopped parsley might be added at the very last, but it is better quite plain.

SANDY POTATOES

Pommes sablées make a favourite dish in France. They should be more common here, for they are both simple, decorative, and unusual. The potatoes should be pared and then cut in dice of about one-inch sides. They must then be fried slowly in shallow butter, and, when both sides are golden, some white breadcrumbs are added towards the end and cooked with them. The crumbs adhere to the potato dice, with the result that they are as if sandy when done.

PEACH DUMPLINGS

Imported Empire peaches can usually be bought this month, and so we can try this attractive-sounding American dish. Make a shortcake mixture as follows. Mix together

Fc 81

two cupfuls of flour (cups are as near breakfast-cups as anything), four teaspoonfuls of baking powder, half a teaspoonful of salt, and a tablespoonful of sugar. Sift these twice to mix them well, work in a quarter to a third of a cupful of butter with the tips of the fingers, and gradually add three-quarters of a cupful of milk. Roll this paste out to a quarter of an inch thick, and cut into four-inch squares. Stone the peaches, fill them with sugar flavoured with nutmeg or cinnamon, place them in the middle of each square, dot them over with butter, draw the corners of the paste over the top of the fruit and pinch the edges together. Prick with a fork, and bake in a moderate oven for half an hour. A good idea is to serve Hard Sauce with them. (For Hard Sauce, see p. 207.)

SPANISH FRITTERS

Get a French roll, or indeed any stale white bread, remove the crust, and cut the crumb into rounds as thick as your finger. Soak them in a little cream or even milk, into which you have beaten an egg, seasoned with grated nutmeg, powdered cinnamon, and castor sugar. When they are well soaked, let them dry a little, and then fry them brown in a little butter, and serve them very hot. Hot jam can be handed with them if necessary, but it will probably be found better just to give them the faintest powdering with very fine sugar.

PRUNE SOUFFLÉ

Soak half a pound of prunes and cook them until tender in a very little water. Take out the stones, chop them up very finely, and mash them with a quarter of a pound of castor sugar. Whisk up five whites of egg, and fold them into the prune mixture. Butter a soufflé-dish, put in the prune mixture, and bake in a moderate oven for about ten minutes. Be careful that it is not overcooked, as there is no body in this soufflé. A sauce-boat of whipped cream would be nice, especially if it had had a short while in the refrigerator. But the soufflé must be brought to the table instantly. To add a glass of port wine to the prunes when you are cooking them, or to cook them in a half and half mixture of water and claret or burgundy, will make all the difference.

ROXBURY PUDDING

Another good idea for using up an extra egg-white or two. Here again " cups " are breakfast-cups. Cream half a cupful of butter (it is about four ounces), and add half a pound of sugar gradually, beating well. Then add half a cupful of milk, two and a half cups of flour sieved with three and a half teaspoonfuls of baking powder, a pinch of salt, and four stiffly beaten egg-whites. Put into a greased pudding-basin, and steam for an hour. Then serve with hot chocolate sauce. This is a large pudding : half quantities would be ample for four. But it is quite one of the lightest things I know. A touch of cinnamon in the sauce will do no harm.

ANTIBES TOMATOES

An uncommon and very attractive savoury dish, say for luncheon. Pound up some anchovy fillets with a touch of garlic, a little tinned tunny fish carefully drained of oil, some *fines herbes* (parsley, chervil, chives, and tarragon), and very little breadcrumb soaked in milk and then drained. Scoop out some tomato halves and fill them with this mixture, sprinkle them lightly with salt, pepper, a little chopped thyme, parsley, and (if you have it) fennel, and finally a few drops of olive-oil on each. Bake them in the oven, and serve them on toasts or dainty rounds of fried bread.

CHEESE SOUFFLÉ WITH MAIZE

An Italian recipe which is worth knowing. Put a pint of milk into a saucepan and season it with a saltspoonful of salt. Bring to the boil, and then sprinkle in a couple of ounces of maize flour. Mix, put on the cover, and cook in a very moderate oven for twenty-five minutes. Then, in another saucepan, mix it with an ounce and a half of butter and the same of grated Parmesan cheese, working it well in, add an egg beaten with two egg-yolks, and, finally, three stiffly whisked egg-whites. Pour into a buttered soufflé-dish, sprinkle with grated cheese, and cook in the usual manner.

MAY

THE KITCHEN GARDEN IN
MAY

WHILE we are gathering our first *Asparagus*, we must be thinking of our main crop of *French Beans*, and a few *Runner Beans* may be risked if the weather is favourable. The main crop of *Beetroot* should also be sown now, and a successional sowing of *Broccoli*. These last can be planted out now as often as may be and some of the better grown *Brussels Sprouts* seedlings got out, too. *Cabbage* we must continue to plant out as opportunity offers, and *Cauliflowers* as well. If you like those pleasant *Sweet Peppers*

(*Capsicums*), which are such a feature of Hungarian cookery, they can be sown now for bearing green fruit in the autumn. *Carrots* should be thinned and a few more rows sown for young ones for garnishes later on. *Celery* can be planted out if time permits the trenches to be dug. *Lettuces* must be sown and planted out, as can *Maize* (*Sweet Corn*) and *New Zealand Spinach* which many prefer to the real sort. It has a good flavour, and certainly saves cook trouble. *Peas, Savoys, Turnips* may all be sown. *Tomato* plants for setting out in the open should gradually be hardened off.

NOTES

MAY DISHES

BROCON SOUP

I found this interesting recipe in a nineteenth-century cookery book. Take two good-sized onions and a little ham (or bacon) cut in small pieces, simmer with a little butter until quite brown, mix two tablespoonfuls of flour with this, add a quart of good stock and a sprig of thyme, and let all boil for half an hour, stirring occasionally to prevent burning. Season with salt and a little cayenne, a dessertspoonful of sugar, and a glass of sherry or Madeira. Boil three eggs for ten minutes, get the yolks out, and rub them through a sieve with a little butter, pepper and salt, and a dessertspoonful of flour. Make them into little balls about the size of marbles; let them remain in boiling water over the fire for a few minutes; put them on a sieve and throw them in just as the soup is being served up.

POTAGE SANTÉ

Peel three medium-sized potatoes, quarter them, and cook them quickly in salted water. When they are soft, drain them, rub them through a fine sieve, and mix them with a pint and a half of white stock. Have ready two tablespoonfuls of thinly sliced sorrel leaves just " melted " in butter, add them to the soup, and bind with cream or egg-yolk (or both), finishing with a few tiny bits of butter.

SOUP WITH OMELETTE

Make a clear light consommé, of meat or vegetables, and just before you are ready to serve it up cook a thin savoury omelette (*omelette aux fines herbes*). Be careful not to burn the omelette, but do not fold it; just cut it into very thin strips or small pieces, and add it to the soup just before serving. In my opinion, a little more tarragon than usual in the *fines herbes* vastly improves this soup, especially if it is made with chicken consommé.

ONION OMELETTE

This omelette is best for luncheon, when it can stand as a dish by itself—and an excellent one, too. Cut a medium-sized onion into very thin slices, and fry them golden brown (no more) in a little butter. Drain them well and add them to your eggs before you pour them into the omelette pan. Now make the omelette in the usual way, and serve it garnished with triangular croûtons of fried bread and a rich tomato sauce poured round it. A light sprinkling of very finely chopped fresh parsley on the top completes an attractive dish.

SCRAMBLED EGGS WITH BACON

Cut some thickish rashers of bacon in cubes, and fry them until they are crisp. Take them out of the pan and keep them warm ; add a little more fat if necessary, and in this scramble your eggs in the usual way. This method gives quite an original touch to a stand-by breakfast dish.

EGGS POLIGNAC

Butter some small timbale moulds (small Castle Pudding moulds would do), and powder the inside with some very finely chopped fresh parsley. Shake off any parsley bits that have not stuck to the butter, and into each mould break, very carefully, an egg, letting it slide in so that no air bubbles are made or there will be holes in the finished egg. Sprinkle a little salt and pepper over the egg, and put a dab of butter on each. Now put them into a sauce-pan of hot water, with enough water to come half way up their sides, put on the lid, and let them steam for eight to ten minutes. They should not be hard, but firm enough to stand up when turned out. Serve them turned out on a flat dish, with a white or tomato sauce poured round them. Or they may be turned out, if preferred, on to little rounds of buttered toast, but in this case they should be drained before being placed on the toasts.

EEL MATELOTE

The Mitre at Hampton Court is famous for its Eel Matelote besides its Duck and Green Peas and Lobster Cutlets, and once, over a bottle of Beaune, I induced the chef to part with his recipe. But alas ! I have lost it ; though the following is quite as good. It is well worth the bottle of wine (this time to be used in the dish), I can assure you. Cut the prepared eels into pieces about two or three inches long : there should be about two pounds. Now, in a shallow saucepan or frying-pan (a real French sauté-pan is the best), put your pieces of eel, four ounces of minced onion, a bouquet of parsley, thyme, and bayleaf, a good pinch of salt, and a bottle of red wine. If you take my advice you will also add a small piece of garlic, crushed, the size of a haricot bean. Bring quickly to the boil, pour in a sherry-glassful of brandy, and set it alight. When it has burned out, put on the lid, and boil fairly quickly for a quarter of an hour. Then take the pieces of eel out and keep them warm. Strain the liquor into a basin, rinse the pan in hot water, and pour the liquor back again. Continue to boil it until you have reduced it by a third, then add a small spoonful of flour kneaded with two small " nuts " of butter, and boil for two minutes. Add pepper and a few button onions and mushrooms which you have previously cooked in butter. Put in the pieces of eel, and simmer all together for five minutes. Arrange the pieces of fish on your dish, surround them with the onions and the mushrooms, pour over the sauce (which you have finished with a few bits of butter), and finally set round half a dozen croûtons of fried bread. A dish in a million, and enough for six. Happy six !

SALMON TAIL

This is a good way of cooking Empire imported salmon, and encouraging the use of the herb garden, too. Buy about three pounds of the tail and let it lie for three or four hours in half a gill of olive-oil, a teaspoonful of chopped thyme, two of chopped parsley, and a bayleaf. Turn it three times during this marinading. When the time is up, wipe the piece well, and grill it, basting it with butter. When it is cooked on both sides, serve it with a sauce made of two tablespoonfuls of melted butter mixed with a teaspoonful each of chopped chervil and chives and a couple of teaspoonfuls of lemon juice.

TROUT GRENOBLOISE

This is the famous way of cooking trout in Grenoble. Wipe your trout, flour them, and fry them in a little butter until they are browned on each side. Take them out of the pan and keep them warm, while you let the butter get just a little darker (it should be a light brown), then quickly squeeze some lemon juice into it and add a sprinkling of chopped parsley. Pour this over the fish, and serve them garnished with chopped capers and slices of raw lemon.

RED MULLET MONTESQUIEU
Do not allow the fishmonger to look at you with scorn if you ask him to fillet the red mullet, and, when you get home, have the fillets seasoned with salt and pepper and rolled in melted butter into which you have chopped some chives (or onion) and parsley. Then fry them in a little butter, and serve them with nut-brown butter (*beurre noisette*) seasoned with lemon juice and chopped parsley.

SARDINE PANCAKES
Make some very thin pancakes with a slightly salted batter. Bone, skin, and mash up some sardines, and stuff the pancakes with these. Arrange them in a row in a long dish, and hand with them a sauceboat of thinnish tomato sauce, rather highly seasoned.

TIMBALE OF FISH
Cook some potatoes and mash them well (about a pound and a half). Season them with salt, pepper, and a little grated nutmeg, and beat into them a couple of egg-yolks. Now butter a timbale mould, or a soufflé-dish plentifully, and sprinkle the inside all over with breadcrumbs, white or browned. The dish should be just large enough to hold the potato mixture. Now bake it in the oven for forty minutes, take it out, and cut the top off smartly in one piece, and scoop out the potato inside to leave a wall all round the sides about an inch thick. Paint the inside with white of egg, and put the thing back, case and all, in the oven to dry. Meanwhile make a sauce with an ounce of butter, the same of flour, and enough milk to give it rather a stiff consistence ; season it with salt, pepper, a spot of curry powder, and a good touch of anchovy essence. Now, in this sauce, warm up any left-over white fish you may

have, or open a tin of crab or lobster, and add, if you need
more substance, a few tinned and quartered mushrooms.
Put this into the timbale, put on the lid again, and press
it well down. Now turn the mould upside down on a dish,
and after a few seconds it will turn out perfectly well. It
must, of course, be very hot when served, and here, too,
a tomato sauce does duty very well.

SAUTÉ CHICKEN

Small chickens are so useful nowadays that this recipe
should be welcomed. Cut the little bird into five or six
pieces and brown them in butter. Take them out and put
them into a covered pan with a little more butter, season
them with salt and pepper, add a leaf or two of tarragon,
and let the pieces simmer with the lid on for twenty minutes
or so. Take them out and arrange them on a dish, garnishing them, if you wish, with a few cooked mushrooms, or
asparagus tips, or cauliflowerets. Add some cream to the
pan they were cooked in, stirring and scraping the bottom
well, to loosen the congealed juices from the bird, let this
sauce boil, to thicken slightly, and pour it over the chicken
after testing the seasoning.

CURRIED RISSOLES

Soak in milk two good slices of crustless stale bread, drain
them, and mash them to a fine pulp. Sieve a couple of
tomatoes, and mix their pulp with the bread. Add to this
half a pound of finely minced raw veal or pork, a small
onion, also minced fine, and season with salt, pepper, and
grated nutmeg. Bind with a beaten egg, shape into small
balls, egg-and-breadcrumb them, and fry them brown.
Finally, let them stew slowly in some curry sauce, which
you have made meanwhile according to your own ideas
on the subject.

VEAL A LA CRÉOLE

Cut three pounds of brisket of veal into two-inch squares,
half a pound of lean ham (or bacon) and four medium
potatoes into cubes, and two large onions and two medium

carrots into slices. Melt a tablespoonful of lard in a large stewpan, and fry the veal, seasoned with salt and pepper, until it is brown all over. Then add the other ingredients, with a minced clove of garlic, and brown them, too. Now mix in a tablespoonful of flour, six fresh tomatoes cut in slices, a teaspoonful of vinegar, some chopped parsley, thyme, bayleaf, and marjoram, a little cayenne pepper and a quart of water. Cover closely, and let it simmer for about two hours, when it should be ready to eat with approbation.

SQUABS

Squabs, those succulent baby pigeons, are so good when just plainly roasted that it seems almost sacrilegious to suggest a variation. But if something just a trifle more savoury is needed, this American fashion may meet with approval. They are roasted as usual, but first of all they are stuffed with a mixture of half a breakfast-cupful of breadcrumbs, a third of a cupful of mushrooms cut in pieces, three tablespoonfuls of melted butter, and salt and pepper.

LAMB A LA CATALANE

It should not be impossible to get a good slice of leg of lamb from the butcher—a slice right across the bone—and if this can be done, a pleasantly exotic dish awaits you. It comes from Roussillon in the very south of France on the edge of the Pyrenees. Fry your thickish slice in pork fat after you have seasoned it well with salt and pepper. Then put in the same pan two or three cloves of garlic and a chopped tinned sweet pepper (pimento), and leave it to cook for a few minutes longer. Then sprinkle it with flour, and moisten it with stock or hot water and a glass of dry white wine and a tablespoonful of tomato purée. The liquid should just cover the meat, which you can then cover with the lid and leave simmering in it until it is done, which will depend on the size of the meat. When ready, strain the sauce over it, and serve.

ASPARAGUS A LA CRÈME

A good dish for those who do not want the trouble of eating

their asparagus with their fingers ! First cook the asparagus in the usual way, and, when well drained, cut the soft part of the heads into pieces about an inch long. (It is just as well, by the way, to keep the asparagus rather under-done for the first part of its cooking.) Keep them hot while you melt a piece of butter in a saucepan, add to it plenty of cream, and season with salt, pepper, and, if you like, the tiniest grating of nutmeg. Bring the cream and butter to the boil, then add the asparagus, and shake over the fire for a minute or two longer, until the sauce thickens. Do not stir it or you may break the asparagus pieces. And be sure that those pieces are very well drained and quite dry before you add them to the cream, or the appearance of this attractive dish will be quite spoiled.

FRIED RADISHES

A peculiar accompaniment for lamb, mentioned here because sometimes the radish bed gets a little out of hand and its denizens badly need eating, is fried radishes, as an alternative to turnips. Use up the large ones in this way. Peel them, slice them, boil them for twenty minutes in salted water, and, when they are cooked, drain them thoroughly and fry them in a little butter.

LETTUCE A L'ÉTOUFFÉE

Braised lettuces are excellent, but uncommon. This way is simpler, and perhaps even better. Wash and drain a pound of lettuce leaves, and cut them across in strips of about a finger's width. (I have found myself that in this dish Cos lettuces are better.) Divide an ounce of butter into little pieces. Put a third of the lettuce into a stew-pan which has been previously buttered, put on it a third of the butter, then lettuce and butter until the other two-thirds have been put in in two more layers. In the middle on top put a bouquet of parsley, thyme, and bayleaf, a small lump of sugar, and four small onions. Sprinkle lightly with salt, but do not add any liquid whatsoever. Now cover the pan closely, and let the contents simmer for three-quarters of an hour to an hour. When the lettuce is done, there will be a couple of tablespoonfuls or so of liquid left in the bottom of the pan, and this you can bind quickly with flour and butter and pour over the lettuce, which you will serve with the onions, if you like, but with the bouquet removed.

BRAZILIAN PUDDING

Even those who do not like tapioca will not despise this version of it. Put seven-eighths of a pint of milk into a saucepan with two ounces of sugar, a pinch of salt, and an ounce and a half of butter. When the sugar has dissolved, bring the milk to the boil, and sprinkle in a quarter of a pound of tapioca. Put the pan in the oven with the lid on for twenty minutes, and then, in another saucepan, add to the tapioca mixture three yolks of egg, an ounce and a quarter of butter, and two stiffly whisked egg-whites. Pour this into a mould which you have already lined with caramel, and cook this delicious pudding in a *bain-marie* or covered pan. No sauce should be served with it other than the caramel, which will run down its sides.

FRIED BANANAS

For this banana sweet let the halved bananas lie for a while sprinkled with sugar and lemon juice, and then dip each half in very well whisked egg (white and yolk together), and fry them in clarified butter. They will take about five minutes to cook. Arrange them on a hot dish, bring them swiftly to the table, and almost on the instant of serving, throw over them a small glassful of warmed rum and set it alight.

CRÈME DE NOISETTES

Bring half a pint of milk to the boil, and then, off the fire, add to it four ounces of finely chopped grilled hazel-nuts. Bring to the boil again, put on the lid, and cook thus for a few minutes. Now add four sheets of gelatine, softened in cold water, after the liquid has cooled a little, and add, too, the yolks of four eggs, well mixed, with about a quarter of a pound of castor sugar. Let the mixture thicken quietly on a slow fire, stirring all the time, and then let it get cold.

Then add half a pint of whipped cream, put it into a mould, and leave it on ice or in the refrigerator for a couple of hours before you want it. A delicious sweet.

WOODCOCK TOAST

We all know Scotch woodcock, but Woodcock Toast is not so common. Boil two fowls' (or one goose's) livers, and pound them up to a paste with an ounce of butter, adding a teaspoonful of anchovy essence, a pinch of salt, a raw egg-yolk, and a tablespoonful of melted meat glaze. Stir in also a tiny pinch of mixed herbs and some black pepper, mix well again, and pass through a sieve. Spread this mixture on pieces of toast or fried bread, and put a little buttered egg on top. It is supposed to taste like woodcock, but although I cannot say it does, it is nevertheless very good to eat.

CHEESE FINGERS

Cut some stale white bread into fingers, soak them in cream, and then drain them. Now roll them in very finely grated cheese seasoned with pepper, pressing it on to the fingers with the flat of a knife. Put them in a buttered baking-dish, and bake them in a very hot oven, turning them over once. They should be served very hot.

STUFFED EGGS CARÊME

Hard-boil some eggs and cut them in half. Make a purée of the yolks with a little chopped shallot, parsley, and sorrel. Moisten with a touch of cream if necessary. Stuff the halves with this mixture, set them on pieces of fried bread, and bake them for five minutes.

SMOKED SALMON TOASTS

These are rather good, but a bit expensive, though you can get some cheaper Canadian (I think) smoked salmon which would do for this savoury. Sprinkle some soft herring roes with salt, cayenne and finely chopped parsley, chives and chervil. Wrap each in a very thin slice of smoked salmon, and cook them very gently in butter until the roes are done. Set them then on hot buttered toasts, and serve.

JUNE

THE KITCHEN GARDEN IN
JUNE

D^O not allow the *Asparagus* to be cut too late or the bed will suffer. About the middle of the month as a general rule is the last time for cutting, but there are several days' latitude each way according to your residence, for the more northerly you are, the later you can be. Sow more *French Beans* and *Runner Beans* for a late crop, and plant out the *Capsicums* you sowed last month. See that the *Celery* bed is made, and take precautions against the Celery Fly. Go on sowing and planting *Lettuces*, and particularly sow

Chicory and *Endive* which will be welcome later in the year. Sow more *Spring Onions*, and have a look at the onion bed with a critical eye. Gardeners are often only too fond of growing enormous bulbs which are not only embarrassing by their size, but worse for keeping than the smaller ones. Sow a few more rows of *Peas*, remembering that if you sow them late enough you may be able to enjoy a dish (as I have done) in November, provided that you remember to put on some big cloches before the frosts take them. Towards the end of the month sow *Turnips.*

NOTES

JUNE DISHES

ASPARAGUS SOUP

When asparagus begins to go over, or there is a plethora of those long and lanky heads hardly good enough for the table, then is the time for Asparagus Soup. Take thirty or forty heads, cut off the tips and put them aside, and cut the cleaned stalks into short pieces. Simmer these for half an hour in vegetable stock, potato water being quite the best. Now rub lightly through a sieve, so as to avoid any strings slipping through, heat it up, and, when it boils again, add the tips and seasoning to taste, cooking gently for about ten minutes. Then stir in a gill of cream, and serve with croûtons of fried bread and, if you like, a few very young peas.

GREEN PEAPOD SOUP

Peapods make a nice light soup, satisfying both to the palate and the pocket. Take a quart of the peapods, wash them well, and pull off the inside skin. Put them into two quarts of boiling water with a sprig of mint, a small lettuce, a sprig of parsley, and a small onion. Cook all together until the vegetables are tender, then rub through a fine sieve. Boil the soup up again, season it with pepper, salt, and a pinch of sugar, and add half a pint of milk. A spoonful or two of cream will help to enrich this very cheap soup, and a few little peas will act as a pleasantly deceptive garnish. Tiny croûtons of fried bread, too, if you like.

SORREL SOUP

The Hind's Head Hotel at Bray is famous for its Sorrel Soup. Here is a good way of making it. Pick over half a pound of sorrel, removing the ribs and damaged leaves, chop them up coarsely, and stew them slowly with a small piece of butter in a covered pan for twenty minutes. Do not be disturbed at the change their colour will undergo, they will taste just as good. Sprinkle over a good table-spoonful of flour, and cook this a little. Now moisten with just over a quart of hot water, and season with salt and a pinch of sugar. Cover, and boil gently for a quarter of

107

an hour. Now beat up two whole eggs and mix them with the soup, pouring them through a strainer. The soup must not boil after the eggs have been added. An excellent soup, and good for summer-time, too.

ŒUFS MOLLETS

Œufs Mollets, or soft-boiled shelled eggs, are uncommon enough to surprise some of our friends and please ourselves at the same time. There are a very large number of ways of presenting them : here are half a dozen, all admirable for a rather dressy luncheon-party.

To cook the eggs to perfection, they should be plunged into boiling water and cooked for five and a half to six minutes, no more. Put them into cold water and shell them. If necessary, they can be kept when shelled in moderately salted hot water until wanted, not hot enough, of course, to cook them further. All the following recipes are cooked in tartlets, made of a size to fit the eggs.

Œufs mollets à l'Argenteuil. Lay some cooked asparagus tips in the bottom of the tartlet, then the egg on top, and cover it with a cream sauce mixed with a purée of green asparagus tips.

à la Chasseur. First garnish the tartlets with fried slices of chicken's liver bound with Chasseur sauce. The egg is masked with the same sauce. (If you do not wish to make your own sauce, an excellent Chasseur sauce is bottled by Escoffier.)

à la La Vallière. The egg is set in a tartlet on a bed of sorrel *à la créme* (cooked in the same way as spinach), masked with Supreme sauce, and decorated afterwards with asparagus tips.

à la Milanaise. The tartlets are garnished with macaroni *à la milanaise*, the egg is coated with Mornay (cheese) sauce, which is quickly browned before coming to table.

à la Rossini. A slice of *foie gras*, lightly fried in butter, adorns the bottom of the tartlet. The egg is covered with Madeira sauce, and surmounted by a slice of truffle.

à la Stanley. An onion purée flavoured with curry goes at the bottom of the tartlet, and a creamy curry sauce is poured over the egg.

FRICASSÉE OF PRAWNS

An excellent fricassée can be made by cooking for a quarter of an hour or so some lightly fried prawns in a good Béchamel or white sauce, in which fish stock will have taken some part if possible. Finish, off the fire, with the yolk of an egg beaten in a little lemon juice. Cayenne pepper, in moderation, would be a pleasant addition, and so would some freshly chopped parsley.

LOBSTER NEWBURG

A summer dish, indeed, suitable, if circumstances permit, of an exercise on the chafing dish. Make it, if cheapness is a consideration, with those crawfish tails euphemistically called Cape lobster. Cut the lobster, or the tails, in pieces, and put them with an ounce of butter in a pan large enough to hold them all on the bottom. Fry them for five or six minutes, turning them over once (the reddish skin of the lobster will impart a rosy tint to the butter and eventually to the sauce), then add enough sweetish sherry or Madeira nearly to cover them, put on the lid, and cook quickly so that in about fifteen minutes the wine will have reduced to about three spoonfuls. Now pour in a mixture of four yolks of egg and a gill and a half of cream, and shake this gently (do not stir it) over the flame until it gradually thickens and gets like a pinkish custard. The moment for serving has then arrived, and if you like to eat some plainly boiled and well-dried rice with it, then do so.

FRIED RICE WITH CRAB

This is a Chinese dish called *Hye Yook Chow Fan*, as I am told. Put six ounces of finely shredded crab and three well beaten eggs into a hot oiled pan, and cook for one minute. Add two pounds of cooked rice, salt and pepper to taste, and a few drops of Soya sauce, and cook for three minutes with frequent turnings. Add one ounce of spring onions cut very fine, and cook for half a minute.

SPELDERED HERRINGS

I am obliged to the Herring Book for this recipe. Scale and clean the fish, remove the heads and tails and backbone. Lay them on a dish, dust them with cayenne, squeeze lemon juice over them, put a nut of beef dripping on each, and grill them. Serve with cut lemon.

GUINEA FOWL AUX CHOUX

Guinea fowl are getting a bit older, so this recipe may prove useful. First brown the guinea fowl (five minutes) in lard in a casserole or an oval pan. Take it out, and put into the pan a third of your cabbage, which has been blanched for ten minutes and well dried, and on this the guinea fowl. Cover it with another layer of cabbage. Now add some cubes of blanched pickled pork, an onion stuck with two or three cloves, and a bouquet of parsley, thyme, and bayleaf. Finish with the rest of the cabbage, and pour in some good well flavoured stock, to come up nearly to cover the cabbage. The best stock to use is that from which the fat has not been removed, as this adds richness to the cabbage. Now bring to the boil on top of the stove, cover the pan with greased paper, and put on the lid. Put into a very moderate oven, and simmer for an hour and a half to two hours.

STUFFED LETTUCE LEAVES

Mince a pound of raw beefsteak, and boil a gill of rice in milk. When the rice is cold, beat up an egg in a little milk, and add to it the beef, salt, and pepper. Take a good spoonful of this mixture and wrap it up in a lettuce leaf, repeating this until you have used it all. Tie the lettuce leaves with cotton, and brown them all over in butter. Cover them with some good well flavoured stock, and cook them very slowly in the oven for two hours.

SAUCISSES AU VIN BLANC

The thinnish sausages called " Parisian " are best for this dish. Blanch the sausages for a moment in boiling water, prick them lightly, and fry them. Strain off the fat and, for every twelve sausages, pour over them a glass of dry white wine. Let this slowly reduce to half, while in another pan you make a sauce with butter, flour, and a breakfast-cupful of stock. Add the wine to this, and at the last minute bind with a yolk of egg. Pour it over the sausages, and serve them in a circle of mashed potatoes.

BRAISED DUCKLING WITH GREEN PEAS

Cut up six ounces of streaky pickled pork into large dice, blanch them in boiling water, dry them, and fry them in butter. In the same fat brown fifteen or so button onions. Take them out, and keep them warm while you fry the duckling in the same butter. When it is nice and brown take it out, pour off the fat, and swill the pan with a little brown stock. Now put back the duckling with the pork and onions, a pint and a half of shelled peas, a bouquet of parsley, thyme, and bayleaf, and half a pint of half-glaze (*demi-glace*) sauce. Let the whole thing braise until the duckling is done ; then take out the bouquet, reduce the sauce until it only just covers the vegetables, and serve.

FRITTO MISTO

I am indebted to Countess Morphy's *Good Food From Italy* for the following recipe for *Fritto Misto à la Fiorentina*. " These delicious dishes of fried ingredients," she says, " served on the same plate are typically Italian and are slightly reminiscent of the English mixed grill, but the Italian *fritto misto* is much lighter and daintier. The Florentine one consists of minute potato croquettes, calf's brains, sweetbread, both in very small proportions, small globe artichokes, small pieces of marrow, very small lamb cutlets, all dipped in flour, seasoned with salt and pepper, then coated with beaten yolk of egg and fine white breadcrumbs. All these ingredients are fried in a deep pan of very hot oil to a golden colour." Drain well, and serve on a very hot dish, or on the plates themselves.

BEETROOT PURÉE

As a change from hot cubes of beetroot liberally buttered and sprinkled with parsley, let me suggest this for the nice young beetroots. Boil them whole, and, when they are done, put them through a potato masher—after skinning them, of course ! Add about an ounce of butter, a teaspoonful or more of lemon juice, salt, pepper, and a tablespoonful or so of cream. A delicious purée that is surprisingly little known.

YOUNG BROAD BEANS

A tip once given me by a local greengrocer was to treat your young broad beans as if they were runner beans. That is to say, wash them well, take off the ends, and slice them downwards, but not too finely. Then cook them in boiling salted water with a tiny pinch of sugar. Do not cook them too long or they may get rather floury. They take about as long as runner beans and taste rather like a mixture of them and broad beans. Be sure to butter them nicely, and if you have any left over, you will find them good as a salad with plain French dressing.

PETITS POIS A LA FRANÇAISE

My readers have told me often that a recipe for this dish is sometimes difficult to find. In the first place, for the best results, the peas should be all the same size. Put a pint and a half of shelled peas in a thick enamel saucepan with the heart of a small cabbage lettuce cut in half, a dozen button onions cleaned but not peeled, two and a half ounces of butter, and three lumps of sugar broken into small pieces. Mix these well together, and leave in a cool place with a cover over them for an hour. When you are ready to cook the peas, add half a dozen tablespoonfuls of cold water and a bouquet of four sprigs of parsley tied together with, if possible, a sprig of summer savory. Cover the pan with a soup plate—with half a cupful of cold water in it—so that it fits well down on to the pan. Now put the pan on an even heat, and when its contents come to the boil, move it to the side of the fire (or on to a low flame under an asbestos or other mat). The peas must poach, not simmer. If they cook too fast or too long they will mash. Allow eight to ten minutes for them to come to the boil and twenty-five minutes afterwards. During their cooking, renew the water in the soup plate two or three times (when it begins to get appreciably hot), and shake the pan now and again, but do not stir the peas with a spoon. At the end of this time there should be only about a tablespoonful of liquid left. Two or three minutes before serving take out the bouquet, and put the onions and lettuce on a plate to keep warm. Toss the peas over a flame, so that the remaining liquid reduces, and then add half an ounce of butter in small pieces, shaking it carefully into the peas. Now put them into a dish, and arrange the lettuce and onions around them, so that you can distribute these " extras " among those who like them.

CAULIFLOWER AND POTATO CROQUETTES

Boil some potatoes and pass them through a sieve or potato masher. Boil also some cauliflowers (flowers only), and, having drained and dried them, mix them with an equal quantity of the mashed potato. Moisten this combined purée with a little cream, and season with salt, pepper, and either grated nutmeg or paprika pepper as the mood and the meal find you. Let the mixture get cold (add, if you like, a yolk or two of egg), and shape it into little croquettes, egg-and-breadcrumb them, and fry them in deep fat.

COUPE CLO-CLO

One of the pleasantest of all ices. Break up a few *marrons glacés*, soak them for a little in Maraschino or Kirsch, and then mix them with a vanilla ice cream. In the bottom of each cup put a layer of the *marrons*, cover this generously with the ice cream, and surmount it by a whole *marron* surrounded by a piped border of whipped cream flavoured with strawberry purée.

SWEET CORN PUDDING

Mix three tablespoonfuls of Indian cornmeal with a little cold milk. Boil the rest of the milk (it should be a pint

Hc   113

in all) and add to it the cornmeal, a tablespoonful of castor sugar, and a coffeespoonful of finely grated lemon rind. Cook gently for a few minutes, stirring all the time. Let it cool, and then add two well beaten eggs, and half fill some well buttered cups with the mixture, which should be baked in a moderate oven for half an hour.

COMPOTE OF GOOSEBERRIES

Stewed gooseberries and gooseberry fool are old favourites, but this quite simple compote, which only demands a little Kirsch, is a far greater delicacy. Top and tail a quart of green gooseberries, put them into a saucepan (or better, an earthenware casserole) of boiling water and scald them for a couple of minutes. Now, in another saucepan, make a syrup by boiling half a pound of sugar in a pint of water for ten minutes, then add the drained gooseberries, a tablespoonful of apricot jam, and a liqueur-glassful of Kirsch. Simmer the fruit until tender; let it grow cold in the syrup, and serve as cold as possible. Devonshire cream is strongly recommended with this.

POIRE HÉLÈNE

This simple, but very exquisite, sweet is made by placing a fresh, or tinned, pear on a bed of vanilla ice, and handing *hot* chocolate sauce separately.

MUSHROOM SOUFFLÉ

Chop as finely as possible half a dozen large peeled mushrooms. Melt an ounce of butter, stir into it an ounce of flour, and moisten it with a quarter of a pint of milk. Boil and stir for a few minutes, then beat in three yolks of egg, one after the other, then the minced mushrooms and seasoning to your taste. Then add four well whisked whites of egg, and bake in a soufflé-case in the usual way. The oven should not be too hot ; the case should be put on the floor of it, and the cooking will take abour half an hour. An improvement to my mind is effected by the use of half fresh mushrooms and half bottled or tinned ones. It makes the flavour rather more delicate.

WATERCRESS SOUFFLÉ

Make half a pint of watercress purée, in the same way as you would make spinach purée, and season it with salt, pepper, and, if you like, a very little nutmeg. Put it into a small saucepan, add the yolks of two eggs, and stir over the fire until the mixture thickens. Then let it get cold, and add lightly the whisked whites of three eggs. Put into small soufflé-cases, and bake them for about ten minutes.

FONDUE

A lazy dish for the chafing-dish, but a very famous one. Here is Brillat-Savarin's own recipe for it. Take as many eggs as the number of guests demands, weigh them in their shells, and have ready some grated Gruyère cheese a third of the weight of the eggs and a piece of butter a sixth of their weight. Break the eggs into a casserole and beat them well together, then add the cheese and the butter. Put the casserole on a spirit-lamp (or on a very low heat with an asbestos mat over it), and stir continuously until the mixture thickens. Then add salt and a good deal of pepper. And your *Fondue* is ready. Eat it with a fork, handing dry toast with it.

TOURTE FROMAGÉE

A simple cheese tart which is always acclaimed by visitors. Make a flan of pastry and bake it " blind." When it is cold fill it with the following mixture. Beat well together a quarter of a pound of grated Gruyère cheese, an egg, and a good cupful of cream. Season with a little salt and pepper, and, if you like, a little paprika pepper or a speck or two of cayenne. Bake in the oven for about a quarter of an hour, when the top will be golden and the inside too creamy and delicious for words. A refinement for those who like it is first to rub round the pastry case with a cut clove of garlic, which seems to have a strong affinity to cheese.

JULY

THE KITCHEN GARDEN IN
JULY

WE can still sow a number of vegetables for autumn and early winter use, but only quick-growing varieties must be chosen. *French Beans* and *Cauliflowers* should in this case be sown early in the month, and other crops are *Cabbage, Carrot* (for nice young carrots at Christmas time !), *Corn Salad, Lettuce, Peas, Spinach*, and *Parsley*. But they must not be transplanted, but left where they are sown, being thinned out as soon as they can be handled. Plant out more *Broccoli*, and think about your *Cabbage* for spring eating. If your soil is of the sort in which the cabbages show a tendency to bolt (as mine was where I lived a year ago), it will be better to wait for sowing until next month. Thin out *Cardoons*, and cut down the requisite number of Globe Artichoke plants if you want a supply of *Chards*. Sow more *Endive*, and see that all *Shallots* and *Garlic* are taken. Plant out *Celery* and *Leeks*, make sure that a last sowing of *Parsley* is made, and try a row of early *Dwarf Peas* for your cloches to cover later on. A bed of *Winter Spinach* should be sown, *Turnips* thinned out and more sown, and greens of every description planted out as occasion arises.

NOTES

JULY DISHES

CUCUMBER SOUP

Cut a medium-sized peeled cucumber into thin slices and toss them in butter for a few minutes. Take out and keep warm while you lightly fry a couple of small sliced onions. Now take out the onions and put them and the cucumber into a clean saucepan, and pour enough boiling water over them to make the right amount of soup after it has reduced by a quarter. Season with salt, pepper, a little grated nutmeg, and a tiny pinch of cayenne pepper ; bring to the boil, and simmer for half an hour. At the last moment bind this fresh and delicious soup with two egg-yolks beaten in a tablespoonful or so of cream. You can serve fried bread croûtons with it, if you wish.

SORREL SOUP (COLD)

An experiment worth trying if you want a cold soup for a very hot day. Prepare enough sorrel to leave a pound of the leaves after the ribs and stalks have been removed. Wash it very carefully, and mash and pound it as finely as possible. Then mix it with a pint of thin cream, salt it, and serve it very cold.

CONSOMMÉ MADRILÈNE

This is ordinary cold consommé to which four ounces of raw tomato and an ounce of sweet red peppers (pimentos) have been added for every quart during clarification. It is perhaps worth noting here that cold consommés should be served not as a firm jelly nor a broken-up jelly, as they so often are, but they should be light and easily melting and barely firm.

POACHED EGGS

Some people wonder how you cook those jolly poached eggs that look like round balls and are often served in hotels for breakfast. The secret is to have a deep saucepan with plenty of water. Add salt and a teaspoonful of vinegar, and let the water boil as hard as you can. Now hold the egg near the surface where it is boiling hardest, break it, and drop in the contents all at once. The rapidly moving water will give the egg its round shape, and when it is done, take it out carefully with a perforated spoon. Only one egg should be poached at a time, and it should, of course, be carefully drained before serving. Eggs cooked like this are particularly nice with grilled bacon.

OMELETTE AUX FINES HERBES

This is often a stumbling-block. We all know how to make omelettes, but the *fines herbes* usually gets the worst of it, and mostly consists, so I have found, of chopped parsley and onion. The real *fines herbes* consists of equal quantities of finely chopped parsley, chives, chervil, and tarragon, which, of course, you will have in your herb garden. The amount of *fines herbes* to be added to the omelette (before it is cooked) depends entirely on your own taste, and the size of the omelette.

SALMON CUTLETS

While we are on the subject of herbs, here is a pleasant sauce which calls for fennel. Cut some slices thinly across the salmon, season them with salt and pepper, and fry them as they are in butter. Serve them with the following sauce. Boil a tablespoonful each of chopped fennel, mint, and parsley, and when they have cooked for five minutes, drain them well and chop them finer still. Mix them with half a pint of Béchamel sauce and a little meat glaze, and season them with salt, cayenne pepper, and the juice of half a lemon.

A good sauce, by the way, to eat with *Mackerel* done in the same way, but filleted instead of cut across.

HERRINGS CALAISIENNE

Split the herrings open, bone them, and stuff them with their own soft roes, chopped shallots, parsley, and mushrooms mixed with maître d'hotel butter. Wrap each up in buttered paper, twist the ends securely so as to make the little bags as airtight as possible, and bake them in the oven for about twenty minutes to half an hour. Serve them in the bags.

HERRINGS NANTAISE

Score the herrings in three or four places on each side, flour them, and egg-and-breadcrumb them. Cook them in a little butter until golden on each side, and serve them with a sauce made from their mashed soft roes, flavoured with a little mustard and finished with butter.

TURBOT A LA DUGLÉRÉ

A small turbot is very good when cooked in this way, but fillets or slices can be used, or, indeed, other fish like sole or lemon sole. Put the fish into a shallow fireproof dish which has been well buttered, adding an ounce and a half of chopped onion, half a pound of roughly chopped peeled tomatoes, a pinch of salt, a tiny pinch of pepper, a little roughly chopped parsley, a small wine-glassful of dry white wine. Cover and poach in the oven until the fish is done. Put the fish in a dish while you reduce the liquor in which it was cooked, then thicken it with a couple of spoonfuls of thick white sauce (or, more simply, with flour and butter), finish it with some small pieces of butter and a squeeze of lemon, and pour it over the fish with the vegetables still in it.

PILAFF OF CRAB

Fry a couple of minced onions in butter until they are just golden, add a dessertspoonful of flour, some finely chopped parsley, a fraction of bayleaf and thyme, and as much chopped garlic as your palate allows you, a clove being about the ordinary allowance. Keep on frying for a minute or two, and then add four or five tomatoes peeled and cut in small pieces. Season with a little cayenne, simmer for a quarter of an hour, and then moisten with enough hot stock—about half a pint—and, if you can manage it, a glassful of dry white wine. Have ready about six ounces of Carolina rice which has been boiled for ten minutes and then well drained, and when your stock comes to the boil, throw in your rice and add the flaked flesh of two cooked crabs. Season well (add a touch of curry powder, if you like), cook for about twenty minutes, and serve rather dry but very hot.

FRICANDEAU OF VEAL

This, and the Daube of Beef recommended in September, are both admirable dishes for a picnic or shooting-party. Get from the butcher a slice (or slices) of veal cut from the cushion and cut with the grain of the meat an inch and a half thick. Lard these slices finely on one side. Line a stewpan or casserole on the bottom with thickish rinds of blanched pickled pork or mild bacon, fat side downwards, and on these scatter a large onion cut in slices and a large carrot also cut up. In the middle nestle a bouquet of parsley, thyme, and bayleaf, and on this lay the slices of veal, larded side uppermost. Put on the lid, and let the contents "sweat" over a gentle heat for twenty minutes. Now add half a glass of dry white wine, let it reduce, add the same amount of not too salt stock, let that reduce to a spoonful, and then add more stock just to come to the top of the meat. Cook in a gentle oven for about two and a half hours to three hours. You will know when the veal is done, because it ought to be soft enough to cut with a spoon. As you are going to eat this cold, it is better to see that the gravy has all the grease removed before it is finally poured over the meat in its dish, to set in a delicious jelly.

TRIPE WITH CURRY

Have your cooked tripe cut into convenient pieces, not too small, and let them simmer very slowly for half an hour in a pint of Béchamel sauce which has been flavoured with two teaspoonfuls of curry powder or paste. Then stir in quickly the yolks of two eggs, pour the mixture into a shallow fireproof dish, sprinkle it with breadcrumbs, dot here and there with small bits of butter, and brown quickly under the grill.

CHICKEN A LA CRÉOLE

Cut your chicken up in pieces as if for a fricassée. Melt a couple of tablespoonfuls of butter in a pan, put in your pieces of chicken, and let them simmer there for ten minutes or so without browning. Now put in two chopped onions, and let them brown slightly. Add an inch-cube of lean ham (or bacon) cut finely, and mince up a sprig of parsley and of thyme and a bayleaf. Add here, if you like (and I strongly advise it), half a clove of garlic, also finely chopped. Cook all together for a little while, simmering, then pour in a pint of boiling water, and simmer on a low fire for an hour and a quarter. Twenty minutes before serving add a pint of milk. Serve with lots of green peas.

CHICKEN A LA MARYLAND

This dish when served in restaurants is usually fried chicken accompanied by fried bananas. The recipe given here is a more homely, and possibly more authentic, one. Cut the chicken in pieces, season them with pepper and salt, dip them in flour, then in an egg beaten up with a tablespoonful of water. Then roll them in fine white breadcrumbs, put them in a well buttered baking-dish, and bake them in the oven for about three-quarters of an hour, according to the size of the bird. After five minutes' baking, baste the pieces well with butter and continue to do so. You may find it advisable to put the legs in a little before the rest, as they take slightly longer to cook, if the bird is not a very young one. A creamy white sauce is the right accompaniment, and I strongly suggest new potatoes and a raid on the kitchen garden for some really young vegetables.

BARBECUED GAMMON

Grill a good slice of gammon, letting the fat drop into a pan. When the meat is done, put it into a dish, and add to the fat in the pan three tablespoonfuls of vinegar, a tablespoonful and a half of made mustard, half a teaspoonful of sugar, a little paprika pepper, and a tablespoonful of red currant jelly. Let this sauce heat well through, stir it together, and pour it over the gammon.

PETITS POIS BONNE FEMME

Cut a quarter of a pound of breast of pickled pork in small dice, and blanch them. Fry them in butter with half a pound of button onions. Take out the onions and the pork and keep them warm, and to the butter add half an ounce of flour, and make a white sauce with half a pint of white stock. Add a quart of shelled peas, a bouquet of parsley, the onions and the pork, and let the peas cook in this. The sauce should be reduced by half when the peas are done. Serve it as it is.

AUBERGINES (EGG PLANTS)

A dish of these rich-coloured plants should not be forgotten while they are in season. They make an admirable luncheon dish when stuffed, and if they are plainly fried they offer a good and unusual accompaniment to grilled cutlets or steak. For the latter the aubergines must be peeled and cut into rounds about a quarter of an inch thick. They can then be seasoned, dredged with flour, and fried in butter or in oil. But they are better if a little more trouble is taken over them. After they have been cut in slices, spread them out on a cloth, sprinkle them with salt, cover them with the cloth again, and leave them for an hour. Then press the cloth lightly on to them so as to squeeze out the moisture, dip them one by one into frying batter, and fry them in very hot fat. They should be served at once, well drained.

If you are going to stuff them, do not peel them, but wash them well. Cut off the stalk end and cut them in half lengthwise. Score the cut side fairly often and deeply, and cook them, cut side downwards, in butter or olive-oil until the inside is tender ; which will take about half an hour. Then scoop out the insides, and arrange the shells on a fireproof dish ready for filling. The stuffing can be left much to your discretion. A pilaff rice, a little tomato sauce, some grated cheese, and the chopped-up pulp of the aubergines will make a good dish for a *maigre* day, but if on other days you have some cold lamb or mutton left over, small pieces of this could be added, or it could be used instead of the rice. They are very good when stuffed with their own pulp mixed with some tomato *à la*

128

provençale ; that is, fried in olive-oil with a little garlic and then sprinkled with breadcrumbs and a few drops of oil, and browned in the oven. But whatever way you cook them, they have a pleasant flavour which is all their own and makes them a great favourite with those who know them.

BROAD BEANS

When once the broad beans have been cooked (and here let me say that I am definitely of the opinion that broad beans should be peeled after they have been shelled and before they are cooked), there are one or two amusing ways of serving them. Here are two.

Au lard. Blanch a rasher or two of streaky pickled pork and cut it into very thin strips or small pieces. Fry these lightly in a little butter, sprinkle with a little flour, and moisten with some of the water in which the beans were boiled. Season with salt and pepper and some chopped parsley, or, if possible, chopped summer savory. Put in the beans, cook them in this sauce for a little while, and serve them.

Tourangelle. This is a very pleasant recipe from Touraine. Shell and peel the beans, and cook a pound of them in salted water with a bouquet of parsley and tarragon. When they are done, drain them and keep them warm. Now melt in a saucepan a couple of ounces of butter, and just lightly brown in this a dozen or so spring onions. Add two ounces of lean ham (or bacon) cut in small dice, cook for a minute or two together, and then, off the fire, stir in the beaten yolk of an egg mixed with three or four table-spoonfuls of the water in which the beans were cooked. Add some pepper, a trifle of salt, and a couple of sprigs of chervil, and cook the beans in this sauce for about five minutes, shaking the pan now and then. Take out the chervil on serving, and sprinkle a little chopped parsley over.

BANANA CREAM PIE

Make a flan case of your best pastry, and, when it is cold,

Ic 129

fill it with overlapping slices of banana, sprinkling them as you go with a little lemon juice. Cover these with an ordinary boiled custard, and finish with whipped cream. Coconut can be sprinkled over the cream, and strawberry jam could be added to the bananas, if liked. Also a little rum might be added to the custard, but in that case leave out the jam and coconut.

DUKE OF CAMBRIDGE PUDDING

Line a dish with short crust or puff paste. Now mix together three ounces of warmed butter, three ounces of castor sugar, and two yolks of eggs in a small saucepan. Strew over the pastry inside the tart two ounces of finely chopped candied peel. Now bring the mixture in the saucepan to the boil, and pour it boiling over the peel. Then bake in a rather slack oven until the top is a golden brown.

RASPBERRY CREAM

Pass a pound of raspberries through a hair sieve, and add three or four ounces of castor sugar. Dissolve half an ounce of gelatine in half a teacupful of milk and strain it on to the fruit purée. Then whip up half a pint of cream and fold it into it. Keep cool in a mould till ready to serve as cold as possible.

PRUNE OMELETTE

This will make a good hot-and-cold luncheon dish. Cook half a pound of the best French plums until they are soft, and then rub them through a sieve, seeing that the purée is not too dry. While it is still hot, whisk into it one by one half a dozen whites of eggs. Put the mixture on a long metal soufflé omelette dish, shaping it with a palette knife, and cook for ten minutes in a hot oven. Send quickly to table, and hand at the same time some vanilla ice cream. The flavour of the prunes will depend, of course, on the way you have cooked them. Some prefer to add claret, others port. I am inclined to think the first is better.

CANDIED FRUIT OMELETTE

This is a souffléd omelette, and should therefore be baked in the oven on a metal or glass dish. Beat up six yolks of eggs with some sugar, a pounded macaroon, and a little finely chopped mixed peel and angelica. Add a liqueur-glassful of Maraschino. Whip the whites to a stiff froth, then mix the two together. Shape the omelette on the dish, sprinkle it with powdered sugar, and cook it in a moderate oven for fifteen minutes.

JAM FRITTERS

Cut some rice-paper into rounds of about two and a half inches in diameter, and put in the middle of each a small spoonful of jam. Cover with another round of the paper, and wet round the edges to make them stick together. When well stuck, dip these amusing little cases in batter, and fry in deep fat in the usual way.

PAPRIKA CHEESE CAKES

Grind two ounces of almonds with their skins on, and work them to a paste with six ounces of butter, six ounces of flour, three ounces of grated cheese, a pinch of salt, a teaspoonful of paprika pepper, and the yolk of an egg. Roll out to half an inch thick, brush with beaten egg, and sprinkle with cheese. Bake for fifteen minutes.

HAM AND CHEESE SAVOURY

Cut some rounds of toast, butter them, and on each lay a thin slice of lean ham cut to the same size. Put these in a slow oven while you make some Welsh Rarebit, which you will pour over each of the ham toasts, and serve quickly and hot with a tiny spot of French mustard on the top of each.

AUGUST

THE KITCHEN GARDEN IN
AUGUST

GO on planting out *Broccoli*, and sow *Cabbage*, including *Red Cabbage*. *Cauliflower* sown now and sheltered in a cold frame during the winter will make excellent plants, I have found. Begin to earth up the *Celery*, and you may be able to start blanching your *Cardoons*. Sow winter *Lettuce* (for early spring eating I recommend Winter Density, a curly Cos type), *Endive, Corn Salad*, and *Turnip*. Sow *Onions* thickly, so that you will have plenty of thinnings out for salads and garnishing until the crop is gathered.

NOTES

AUGUST DISHES

A FEW HORS D'ŒUVRE

Everyone knows the simple things like sardines, anchovies, egg mayonnaise, herring fillets in oil, Bismarck herrings, pickled cabbage, potato salad, salade russe, and so on. A prepared dish is sometimes welcome. Here are one or two.

Anchovies and Pimentos are an unusual touch. Arrange thin strips of grilled and skinned pimentos, red or green and tinned if fresh ones cannot be obtained, latticewise with thin fillets of anchovy in oil. Garnish with chopped yolk and white of hard-boiled egg.

French Beans when cold make a good hors d'œuvre, well drained and dressed with French dressing and with the addition of a very little finely cut onion.

Red Cabbage becomes more eatable if you pick out the strips from the pickle and, after draining them well, mix them with thin strips of apple, and mix them with an ordinary French dressing.

Cauliflower Salad. Cut off the flowerets and blanch them in boiling water. Drain them and dry them, and let them lie for a couple of hours in oil and vinegar. Then drain them again, and mask them with a mustard sauce with cream. This is made by putting three tablespoonfuls of mustard in a bowl with a little salt, some pepper, and a few drops of lemon juice. After mixing these well together, stir in by degrees the requisite amount of cream.

Celery Bonne Femme is a mixture of chopped apples and young celery bound with mustard sauce with cream.

COLD MACKEREL

The small mackerel to be had in the shops just now make a delicious cold dish. Either split them, behead and betail them, and poach them in a *court-bouillon* with vinegar, or score them on each side and grill them. But in either case let them get cold, skin them, and serve them covered with mayonnaise sauce to which, if you like, you can add some *fines herbes*, or, better still, just a little chopped parsley and fennel.

A DISH OF SOLE

Torbay sole it actually was, but Dover sole would have been better. It was made impromptu in an emergency, and excellent it was. A fireproof dish with a cover was buttered well, and in it were laid the sole fillets. They were sprinkled with salt, pepper, and a good squeeze of lemon juice; the lid was put on, and the fillets were poached in the oven for about a quarter of an hour. When they were done, the liquid was poured out of the dish into a small saucepan, where it was mixed with about half a teaspoonful of paprika pepper. Half a dozen spikes of chives were then cut thinly into it and about a gill of cream was added. This was boiled gently on the fire until it thickened. Just before the fish was put into the oven, half a cucumber had been cut in rings, and these had been peeled, cut in quarters and had the centre removed. The quarters were cut into match-like strips and they were cooked in boiling salted water while the fish was poaching, and by the time the sauce had thickened, they were done and well drained. The fillets were now arranged on a dish with the pieces of cucumber over them and the creamy sauce, seasoned now, was poured over. A pretty enough dish, and a tasty one, too.

A DISH OF WHITING

Get some small whiting and rub them all over with flour. Melt a nice piece of butter in a frying-pan, and fry the fish slowly until they are cooked, but see that the flour does not colour or the fish get dry. Now for the sauce. Chop up finely some parsley and chives (or the green part of young spring onions), and mix them well (without cooking them) in some well-flavoured stock enriched by a couple of tablespoonfuls of cream. Pour this sauce over the whiting just before they are done, and finish cooking them with it. A light and delicate dish for summer.

FILETS DE SOLES SUZETTE

The first dish for Susan when she grows up. Cut some filleted sole in diagonal strips the width of your little

140

finger, and poach them for about three minutes in some good fish stock, putting them in while it is boiling. Let them drain and get cold, then pile them up in a dish inside a circle of green salad, put one or two little groups of shrimps on the salad and a line of them along the top of the fillets, and cover the whole thing with a creamy mayonnaise sauce flavoured with paprika. If served at another time of year, corn salad should be used for the garnish, but small lettuce would do instead.

BRILL AUX COURGETTES

When there are plenty of little marrows on the marrow bed, then is the time to try this pleasant dish of brill. Fillet the fish and arrange it in a shallow fireproof dish which you have buttered beforehand. Now peel the little marrows (they should be four or five inches long) and cut them in long slices, arrange them over the fish with some peeled and coarsely chopped tomatoes and a pinch of chopped basil. Add salt and fresh black pepper. Now sprinkle over a little lemon juice and then some melted butter, put a buttered paper over the top, and cook in the oven until the fillets are done. Then sprinkle with bread-crumbs and more butter, and brown quickly.

LIVER A LA PROVENÇALE

Cut the liver in slices (lamb's liver for me), season them, flour them lightly, and fry them in olive-oil. Arrange them on a dish and sprinkle with a little parsley. Serve separately some Provençale sauce which you will have made as follows. Peel half a dozen ripe tomatoes, remove the pips, and press out the water. Chop up the red flesh that remains and put it into a saucepan in which you have ready smoking a tenth of a pint of olive-oil. Season with salt and pepper, add half a clove of garlic, crushed, a pinch of sugar, and a teaspoonful of chopped parsley. Cook gently for twenty minutes only, and your sauce is ready.

OLD GROUSE

All shot birds cannot be young ones, and this way of cook-ing an old grouse that comes from Scandinavia may be useful. Tie a slice of larding bacon over the bird, and brown it all over in butter. Add salt and half a teacupful of stock, then a good gill of cream, and cook, with the lid on, until the bird is tender; certainly not less than an hour, more likely two. Baste during the cooking, and, when it is done, serve it with the sauce thickened and handed separately.

TIMBALE OF HAM

A good dish for finishing up the end of a ham. Make a paste with a pound of flour, two ounces of butter, a beaten egg, and a gill of thick sour cream. Cut this into several pieces, roll them out thin, and use some of it to line the sides and bottom of a cake-tin which has first been buttered. Mince up your ham, lean and fat together, but not too much fat, and mince an onion with it, until altogether you have a soup plate full. Now beat up five eggs with half a pint of cream, mix them with the ham and onion, and season with pepper and a little nutmeg, adding salt if necessary. Spread a finger-thick layer of this mixture on the pastry on the bottom of the tin, cover this with a thin layer of pastry, then more mixture, more pastry, and so on until you close the tin with the top layer of pastry. An hour in a hot oven will cook it, and it should be served turned out, with a tomato sauce handed separately. Not really as expensive as it sounds, for remember, it is using up the ham !

TERRINE OF PORK

There is no reason why pork should not be eaten in this way in August, so long as your butcher is reliable, and this terrine makes an admirable stand-by. Cut up in small pieces half a pound of pig's liver, a pound and a half of lean pork, and half a pound of streaky pickled pork. Pass these at least once through the mincing machine, and put it all into a large basin. Now season it well with a finely chopped small onion, a trifle of minced garlic (if you like it), plenty of black pepper, some salt, a good pinch of mixed spice, a grating of nutmeg or a pinch of mace, and a teaspoonful or so of mixed herbs. Now add a good handful of finely grated fresh breadcrumbs, and mix it all up with a well-beaten egg. If it is too stiff, a little stock can be added, but it should be about the same consistence as a Christmas Pudding when ready. Put this into your well-buttered terrine, put a piece of buttered paper right on top of the meat, put on the lid, and bake in a moderate oven for about an hour. It will keep in the refrigerator or ice-chest for some days if a layer of lard is poured over the top after it has got cold and set.

SPINACH CROQUETTES

Boil the spinach in salted water, then drain it, mash it up, and mix it with a beaten egg and a few spoonfuls of grated cheese. Roll this mixture into little sausage shapes, flour them, egg-and-breadcrumb them, and fry them in deep fat. A touch of nutmeg is always an improvement where spinach is concerned.

CORN IN THE COB

Many people grow sweet corn and then wonder what to do with it. Strip off the husk and silky parts. Plunge the cobs into boiling water, put on the lid, and boil for ten or fifteen minutes. Be careful not to salt the water, as it hardens the corn. The best way to eat the corn is with melted butter, sticking a fork into each end of the cob and biting off the corn with one's teeth.

SUCCOTASH

This is a dish of sweet corn and any other beans mixed half and half. The corn is cut from the cob before it is cooked, and it is boiled separately from the other beans. When both done and drained, they are stirred lightly together and mixed with salt, pepper, butter, and, if you like, a little cream.

SPINACH SALAD

Season finely chopped cooked spinach with lemon juice and pack it solidly in small oiled moulds, e.g. a Castle Pudding mould. Chill them, turn the spinach out, and serve on lettuce with a round of lean ham beneath each spinach mould. A Tartare sauce should be handed with this American form of salad.

SEAKALE BEET

This (to me) uninteresting vegetable has many devotees who have tasted it in Switzerland, where, under the name of *Blette*, it is very popular. It can, of course, be eaten plainly boiled and with melted butter like Seakale, but the following two ways do help it a little, I think.

Boil and drain the stems well, and put a layer of them in a shallow fireproof dish which has been rubbed with olive-oil. Pour over them a little stock, season with salt, pepper, and grated nutmeg, and sprinkle over some cheese and chopped parsley. After arranging three or four layers in this way, pour over about a gill of cream beaten with one or two yolks of egg, spread with some breadcrumbs, and brown quickly in the oven.

For the other recipe, drain and dry the cooked stems, and toss them lightly in a frying-pan with a good piece of fresh butter. Add salt and pepper, some grated cheese, and a little meat gravy. Just before you are ready to serve them, beat up a couple of eggs, pour them over the beets, and stir until just set. Serve very hot.

GRATIN DE COURGETTES

Take some small marrows about three inches long, scrape them lightly, chop them up finely, and put them into a wide saucepan with just enough water to prevent their catching, about a tablespoonful. Add a pinch of salt, and stir and cook them until all the water has evaporated. Then add a little butter, some thin cream, grated cheese, and one egg. Mix, pepper lightly, and pour into a shallow fireproof dish. Sprinkle liberally with grated cheese, dot with butter, and brown quickly in the oven.

CUSTARD MARROWS

A well-known writer on cooking vegetables has dismissed these marrows rather summarily as floury and tasteless.

They must have been too large, for if they are picked at the right time they are delicious. Nothing could be nicer than a whole dish of these little fellows, none larger than an inch and a half in diameter, carefully boiled and drained, and dressed with melted butter like new potatoes. And when they get just a little older and are the size of an ordinary jam tartlet, they can be not only nice but extremely decorative, too. In this case you must boil them very carefully, and when they are just done, take them out, and carefully scoop out their insides, leaving a case which, from its shape and indentations, does really look like a tartlet. Now fill this cavity with a mixture of young vegetables—peas, beans, carrots, turnips—and use these pretty little marrows for garnishing, say, a dish of lamb. But see that the vegetables are all cooked separately, as they are much better so. If absolutely necessary, the peas and beans could be cooked together and the carrots and turnips, but they are better apart. One or two very tiny onions might be added, too.

CABBAGE BALLS

An original form of vegetable garnish. We have spoken of stuffed lettuce leaves (cabbage leaves can be stuffed with meat in the same way, but they must be blanched first), and now here is their older cousin. Parboil the cabbage only, so that the outer leaves can be handled without breaking them. When the cabbage is thus cooked, let it drain and get cool. Now take off as many outside leaves as you want cabbage balls, and chop up the rest of the cabbage, discarding the hard bits and seasoning it nicely with pepper and salt. Put some of this chopped cabbage in the middle of each of the leaves, form into a ball, tie with thread, and braise them in good stock.

You can make a luncheon dish of balls like this, if, in addition to the cabbage, you put inside, in the very middle, a little ball of sausage-meat or some kind of forcemeat or mince. In that case you could serve them in a rich sauce or gravy.

Kc   145

POTATOES WITH CHIVES

Boil some potatoes, and mash them in the usual way with butter and some extra pepper. Then, instead of moistening them with milk, use some sour cream, and while doing this whip in some finely chopped chives, or, if your herb garden does not possess these, some very fine green of young spring onions. A good dish with mutton and lamb.

CRÈME BRULÉE

Put into a pint of cream one ounce of sugar, a stick of cinnamon, a small piece of lemon rind. Bring slowly to the boil, and add, off the fire, eight well beaten and strained yolks of egg. Do this by degrees, whipping all the time, but on no account allowing the mixture to boil. Now pour it into a shallow fireproof dish, and bake it like a custard either in a *bain-marie* or a pan of hot water in the oven. When it is cooked, let it get quite cold, then cover it with a thick layer of castor sugar. Put the dish under the grill (or use a salamander, if you have one), and brown the sugar so that it caramelises. Put it by to cool, and decorate it, if you like, with whipped cream, but its severity as it is makes its beauty.

TÊTE DE NÈGRE

Make some vanilla-flavoured cream of rice, and let it get cool. Mix in a couple of tablespoonfuls of thick cream, put it all into a water-rinsed pudding-basin, and let it get quite cold. Turn it out when wanted, and mask it with a chocolate sauce, which you can easily make by melting three ounces of grated chocolate with a spoonful of warm water and a piece of butter the size of a small hen's egg. When this is cold, whip up some cream stiffly, and arrange it like a turban on the Nigger's Head.

CHOCOLATE SOUFFLÉ (COLD)

Dissolve two ounces of chocolate in a gill of milk, and, over a pan of boiling water, whip this with three yolks of eggs and three ounces of castor sugar until the mixture is thick and light. Then add a flavouring of vanilla, a couple

146

of ounces of finely pounded French Almond Rock, and half an ounce of gelatine dissolved in half a gill of water, or, if possible, in half a gill of sweet white wine. Now add up to half a pint of whipped cream and, lastly, the stiffly beaten whites of the three eggs. Have ready a perfectly dry soufflé-dish, and tie a band round it to project two or three inches above the top. Pour in the mixture so that it reaches about an inch and a half to two inches above the top of the dish, let it get cold, and when it is set, carefully remove the band. If you wish, you can leave out the almond rock, but it certainly does improve the soufflé.

SHERRY CREAM

Cook a pint of cream with a well beaten egg-yolk, three tablespoonfuls of sweet sherry, a touch of grated lemon rind, and enough sugar to sweeten it as you like it ; cook these all in a double saucepan, or over a very gentle heat. Keep stirring all the time, and when the mixture assumes the consistence of thick cream, take the pan off the fire, and continue to stir until it is cold. It should then be poured into glasses and kept slightly iced until wanted.

THREE PRUNE SAVOURIES

(1) Cook the prunes, not too well, in unsweetened water after having soaked them, and remove the stones. Now stuff them with finely flaked, cooked, smoked haddock, put them on little toasts, and heat them through in the oven. Sprinkle with paprika pepper before serving.

(2) Treat in exactly the same manner, but stuff them with a mixture of breadcrumbs, grated cheese, and beaten egg.

(3) Roll each cooked, stoned prune in a very thin rasher of streaky bacon, stick a cocktail stick or a tiny skewer through each, and either bake, or, better, grill them. Serve on toasts.

HERRINGS' ROES DE LUXE

Cook some soft herrings' roes in a little dry white wine with a pat of butter, and when they are done, drain them, and season them with salt and pepper. Mix some mustard with butter and spread rounds of toast with it. Put a roe on each and sprinkle with chopped parsley and chives. French mustard is here preferable to English.

SEPTEMBER

THE KITCHEN GARDEN IN
SEPTEMBER

THERE is plenty to do to keep the garden tidy, so perhaps it is as well that other demands are not too great this month. See to the *Strawberry* bed, for putting out plants should not be delayed. Plant out *Cabbages*, and sow more *Cauliflower*, this time in a frame. Sow *Lettuces* in the open and in a frame, and thin out *Spinach* and *Parsley*. If you cover the latter at the end of the month with long cloches, leaving it protected but with plenty of air, you will have a good supply through the winter. *Celery* must again be

151

earthed up, and the blanching of *Chards* begun. Plant out some of the *Endive,* and see that work is well ahead in getting in the *Potato* crop.

NOTES

SEPTEMBER DISHES

MUSHROOM SOUP

Peel half a pound of mushrooms and cut them up. Slice an onion, and put this with the mushrooms into a pint of water, seasoning to taste. Simmer this slowly for half an hour, then rub the mushrooms and onion through a sieve, and return them to the strained liquor. Make a *roux* by mixing four tablespoonfuls of butter with an equal amount of flour, moisten with the mushroom liquor, and stir in a cup of cream on serving.

POTAGE COMPIÈGNE

Make a good purée of haricot beans in the usual way, having boiled them with a small onion stuck with a clove, a little carrot, and a bouquet of parsley stalks. Dilute this purée with hot milk and some of the water the beans were cooked in. Melt some sorrel, cut in thin strips, in a little butter, and put these strips in the bottom of the tureen, keeping them warm while you thicken the soup with egg-yolk and milk. Pour the soup over the sorrel, and garnish with tiny leaves of chervil.

POTAGE LORRAINE

Slice up eight or nine carrots with an onion and a head of celery, and put them into a stewpan with a quarter of a pound of butter and five ounces of soaked and drained haricot beans. Let them stew gently with the lid on for about an hour, and then moisten with three pints of stock, and let the soup then boil gently for an hour and a half. Sieve it, then, and serve it.

HOT CRAB

Here is a simple American fashion. Put a layer of the soft part of the crab in the bottom of the cleaned shell, then cover this with a layer of pounded water or cream cracker biscuits. On this arrange the fleshy part of the claws, pouring over a spoonful of mushroom ketchup. Sprinkle over some hard-boiled yolks of egg roughly chopped, season with salt, black pepper, and a little cayenne, smooth over this the rest of the soft part of the crab, brush

155

with beaten egg, and sprinkle liberally with more biscuit or breadcrumbs. Dot with a few pieces of butter, and bake it in the oven for twenty minutes to half an hour. Needless to say, it should be served very hot indeed.

BRILL WITH POTATOES

For this dish you will want twice as much filleted fish as potatoes. Peel and cut the potatoes into dice, melt some butter in a frying-pan, and fry in it the pieces of potato until they are golden all over. While they are cooking, cut the brill into small pieces, season them with salt and pepper, and flour them, and then fry them until tender and lightly browned with the potatoes. Drain them both and arrange them on a dish. Now squeeze a little lemon juice over them and sprinkle them with parsley, or send them to the table quite plainly and hand a well flavoured tomato sauce with them. The first way is the better and, if you like to, add to it, at this time of year, a few freshly gathered fried button mushrooms ; it will be all the nicer for them.

SOLE ARLÉSIENNE

Poach the sole, whole or filleted, in fish stock, take it out, and keep it warm. Let the stock reduce a little, and then add to it a little chopped onion fried in butter, two roughly chopped tomatoes without skin or pips, a tiny piece of garlic, and some chopped parsley. Cook with the lid on for a few minutes, and then add a dozen olive-shaped pieces of cooked vegetable marrow. Pour this over the sole, and garnish each end of the dish with a small heap of fried onion.

DAUBE OF BEEF A LA PROVENÇALE

For about six people buy two or three pounds of beefsteak, fillet or rump, cut it into thin slices, and beat them well. Get also a pound of pork, half fat and half lean, and mince it very finely, or get the butcher to do so. Put the first slice of beef on a board, season it with salt, pepper, a little finely chopped onion (or onion salt), and a pinch or so of mixed herbs, preferably fresh. On

156

this place a layer of the pork mincemeat, and on this a thin rasher or so of streaky bacon or pickled pork, enough to cover the mince. On this another slice of beef, repeating the process until all the beef, etc., is used up, ending with a slice of beef. Tie this up well with string, and brown the piece all over quickly in butter and olive-oil, half and half. Now put it into a stewpan very little larger than itself, and with it put an onion cut in half, a couple of carrots cut in slices, a calf's foot split in two, a clove of garlic, a bouquet of parsley, thyme, and bayleaf, salt, pepper, a grating of nutmeg, a claret-glassful of dry white wine, the same of water, and a tablespoonful of tomato purée. Put a sheet of greaseproof paper over the top, then the lid, and cook very slowly for about three hours. When done, take out the beef and put it in a long shallow dish. Pour the sauce into a basin, and, when it is cold, remove the fat from the surface. Warm it slightly again, and pour it over the beef. It will be, when cold, a luscious jelly.

A grand dish for a picnic or a September shooting luncheon, after the hot stubble. It can also be eaten very satisfactorily when hot, but it is not so good, I think.

PARTRIDGE AUX CHOUX

Line a casserole or stewpan with rashers of bacon, blanch some cabbage by boiling it for ten minutes, then take it out of the pan, leave it in cold water for five minutes, drain it very well, pressing as much moisture as you can from it with your hands, and put it into the lined stewpan with a seasoning of salt and pepper, a small onion with a clove in it, and a bouquet of parsley, thyme, and half a bayleaf. Meanwhile brown two old partridges all over in butter, and now bury them in the cabbage, cover with a few more rashers of bacon, add a couple of cupfuls of good stock, put a piece of buttered paper over, then the lid on the pan, bring to the boil, and cook very slowly indeed for at least two hours. Half an hour before you want this dish, put in a few small sausages and a grating or so of nutmeg.

Serve the cabbage in a heap with the sausages and birds, cut in halves, upon it.

To taste this dish to perfection, the two old birds should be discarded after they have given their flavour to the cabbage, and their place taken in the final dish by two young birds roasted and halved.

PARTRIDGES EN CASSEROLE

(1) Season your birds inside and out with salt and pepper, and brown them all over in butter or lard. In the bottom of the casserole put a few bacon bones and some button onions which have first been fried in butter. Cover the pan, after putting in two or three spoonfuls of stock, and the partridge or partridges, put on the lid, and cook quietly for about an hour and a half. Then add a couple of glasses of burgundy and some quartered mushrooms previously fried a little. Finish cooking for another half-hour, and serve in the same casserole with the strained gravy poured over the birds.

(2) Cut some cubes of lean bacon, and fry them for about twenty minutes with chopped onion and carrot. Do not let them brown ; let them stew rather. Now stuff the old partridges with sausage-meat, put a piece of fat bacon over each, and brown them all over in butter. Put them in the casserole with carrot, onion, bacon, and a few spoonfuls of good stock, and a seasoning of salt and pepper. Cover closely, and cook for at least two hours. Serve as they are.

STUFFED MARROW RINGS

Peel the marrow, cut it in rings about an inch and a half thick, remove the pips, etc., and leave the rings, sprinkled with salt, on a sieve for half an hour. Then boil them for a quarter of an hour, drain them very well indeed, and arrange them in a large shallow fireproof dish which you have buttered well. Fill the rings with whatever meat stuffing or forcemeat you like, and, when they are stuffed, pour over each a little gravy or tomato sauce. Sprinkle them with breadcrumbs, dot with a little butter, and bake for about ten minutes in a hot oven.

POTTED PIGEONS

Wood pigeons are a problem not only to the farmer but to the cook, too. A dull bird, if ever there was one, but not so bad if potted in this way. Season them well, inside and out, with a mixture of spices according to your fancy. A mixture of cayenne pepper, black, freshly ground pepper, ginger, cinnamon, mace, nutmeg, and salt is as good as any. You must then butter thickly the bottom of an earthenware casserole, put the pigeons in it breast downwards, packing them together as closely as possible, put a good deal more butter round them and over them, a piece of buttered paper over the jar and the lid tightly over that, and bake them until they are tender, which, for young birds, will be about an hour. Take them out, and, while they are still warm, scrape the flesh off them and put it into a terrine, pressing it down fairly tight. Let the liquid remaining in the casserole get quite cold, then remove the butter, being careful to scrape off from it any vestige of gravy adhering to it, melt it down again, and pour it over the pigeon flesh in the terrine. When this is cold, seal it with clarified butter. These pots will keep for some weeks in a cool place, and more or less indefinitely in a refrigerator. The stock which was under the butter will, of course, be priceless for making other dishes, as it is rich and spicy.

GIBELOTTE OF RABBIT

People who live in the country usually despise the rabbit as an article of food ; but this dish may convert them a little. As bunny usually comes to the kitchen for nothing more than the cost of a cartridge, and often not even that, a glass of wine may perhaps be afforded on him this time. Cut the rabbit up in pieces, and fry them until they are half done, in pork or bacon fat. Fry also a few chopped shallots or onions in the same fat, and mix them with the pieces of rabbit. Add some chopped parsley, salt, and pepper, and a glass of dry white wine, preferably Sauterne. Simmer all together for half an hour or so, when it will be ready.

MARROW A LA LYONNAISE

Just as you can make lyonnaise potatoes by frying sliced, cooked potatoes with thinly sliced onion, so you can fry some onion rings in butter, and when they are getting done add some well drained cold strips of parboiled marrow. Toss them both together until golden brown, and serve sprinkled with chopped parsley.

TOMATO FONDUE

Cut three-quarters of a pound of ripe red tomatoes in halves, remove pips and juice but leave on the skin, and chop them up. Put them into a saucepan with a tiny piece of crushed garlic, two parsley stalks broken in half, a tiny sprig of thyme, and a piece of bayleaf as big as your finger-nail. Season with a pinch of salt and pepper and a lump and a half of sugar. Cover, and cook very gently indeed for half an hour. Pass the purée through a fine sieve, put it back into the saucepan, and cook on, this time over a flame, stirring all the time, until it reduces to the right thickness. A leaf or two of fresh basil or a pinch of the dried sort if you have it improves the flavour vastly.

TOMATO FRITTERS

Small tomatoes, if they are not too ripe, make pleasant little fritters. Leave them in boiling water for a few seconds, then skin them. Having made a batter with a quarter of a pound of flour, a tablespoonful of olive-oil, and the whites of two eggs beaten up, coat the tomatoes with this, and fry them in deep fat.

CARROTS AU GRATIN

Cut six large carrots in quarters, and blanch them for half an hour; then drain them and finish cooking them in stock. Pass them through a sieve, keeping them warm the while, season the purée with salt and pepper, sprinkle in a good pinch of flour and one or two tablespoonfuls of the liquor in which they were cooked. Now add separately three yolks of eggs and six well-whisked whites, mix well together, and pour the mixture into a shallow fireproof dish, well buttered beforehand. Bake in a moderate oven for a quarter of an hour, and serve as quickly as possible.

POMMES DAUPHINOISE

Peel and slice your potatoes thinly, and arrange them in layers in a fireproof dish which you have first rubbed round with a cut clove of garlic and then well buttered. Sprinkle each layer with salt, pepper, and a little nutmeg. When the dish is getting full, pour in a pint of milk into which you have beaten an egg and a couple of ounces of Gruyère cheese. Sprinkle the top with more grated cheese, and cook in a moderate oven for about an hour, when the top will be a beautiful golden brown.

BONDE PIGE

A Swedish sweet, and a good one. Crumble some stale brown bread, spread it on a baking-tin, and bake it in the oven with butter and a little sugar sifted over it. Stir it now and again to keep the crumbs separate, and keep your eye on it or it may burn suddenly. While it is still hot, spread a layer in a dish, cover it with a layer of thick apple purée, then with raspberry jam and then more of the crumbs. Repeat these layers, and, when the sweet is cold, cover the top with plenty of whipped cream.

SEMOLINA AND CANDIED PEEL PUDDING

Boil up a pint and a half of milk and sprinkle in just under half a pound of semolina, stirring all the time. Cook for three or four minutes, then turn the mixture into a bowl and add two ounces of butter and four tablespoonfuls of sugar. Let it get cool, then mix in one by one five yolks and one whole egg and a little finely grated lemon peel. Meanwhile you will have soaked in a wine-glassful of rum, a handful of sultanas and some chopped candied peel. Add the well-whisked whites to the pudding and then the fruit and what is left of the rum. Mix well, and pour into a large mould which has first been buttered and then sprinkled with sugar. The mixture should three-quarters fill it. Bake in a moderate oven for about three-quarters of an hour. Serve with strawberry or apricot jam sauce.

ONION TART

Mince up half a dozen onions, and cook them slowly in butter without browning them. If you like, add some cubes of raw bacon, and fry these with the onions. Drain off the butter, let the onions get cool, and then mix them with two whole eggs beaten in a small cupful of milk or cream, and season with salt and pepper. Mix well, and pour into a plate lined with pastry, and bake in the oven for about half an hour.

DUCK'S LIVER TOASTS

Fry the livers in a little butter, and, when they are cold, cut them up and pound them to a paste with a little butter, salt, pepper, and perhaps a little cream. Add just a few drops of brandy, or even of dryish sherry, and heap up this preparation on small pieces of buttered toast which you have spread with the thinnest possible layer of French mustard. Heat them quickly through in the oven.

DEVILLED PRAWNS

Cut up a dozen fresh or tinned prawns into small pieces, sprinkle them with cayenne pepper, and mix with them a dessertspoonful of chutney, a little melted butter, and a spoonful of tomato ketchup. Mix, and heat over the fire, adding a spot of French mustard, then put the mixture on pieces of buttered toast, and serve them quickly.

TOMATO JELLY GARNISH

This recipe is rather unusual so perhaps valuable. It makes a pleasant garnish for salads. Cook some tomatoes with a clove, a pinch of sugar, and half a teaspoonful of chopped onion, and, when they are done, press them through a cloth. To every pint of tomato juice add half an ounce of dissolved gelatine, stir until the mixture cools, and then leave to set on ice or in a cool place.

OCTOBER

THE KITCHEN GARDEN IN
OCTOBER

PLANT out *Cabbages*, if there are still any seedlings left; blanch *Cardoons*; dig and store in sand *Carrots* and some of the *Celeriac*. Continue to earth up the *Celery*, and store *Chicory* for blanching. Blanch *Endive*. Plant out *Lettuce*, and make a last sowing in a frame. Dig and store *Beetroot*, *Salsify*, and *Turnip*, and see that there is a stock of bracken or other protective litter for the *Parsnips* and the *Celery* bed in frosty weather.

NOTES

OCTOBER·DISHES

RIZZO FIGATINI

Make some chicken consommé flavoured with celery, bind it with a yolk of egg beaten up in a little cream, and garnish it with slices of chicken's liver tossed in butter. Hand grated cheese separately.

POTAGE PARMENTIER

Peel a pound of potatoes and cut them in quarters. Cut the white part of three leeks in thin slices, and fry them until they are soft, but not at all browned, in a little butter. To them add the potatoes and a pint and a half of hot water. Season with salt, put on the lid, bring to the boil, and boil quickly for twenty minutes or so. When the potatoes are soft, pass them through a wire sieve, rinse the saucepan, put the purée back into it, bring just to the boil, and simmer very gently for five minutes. Correct the seasoning, adding pepper, take the pan off the fire, stir in two egg-yolks beaten up with a little milk or cream, and add at the last a few small pieces of butter. Serve very hot, with croûtons of fried bread.

HERRINGS A LA PORTIÈRE

Score the herrings once or twice on each side, and dip them in a little milk. Season them with salt and pepper, and roll them in flour. Heat a little butter in a frying-pan, and put in the herrings, frying them on both sides until they are evenly cooked. Now arrange them on a dish, brush them over with mustard, not too stiff, and sprinkle them with chopped parsley. Put some more butter in the pan in which the fish were cooked, and cook it until it colours a little and smells nutty. Pour it quickly over the herrings, pour a dash of vinegar into the pan, and pour this over the fish, too. Serve at once.

OYSTER SAUSAGES

The smaller so-called " sauce " oysters will do for this dish, so it is not as expensive as it looks. It is a good idea for a cocktail-party, by the way. For a pound of veal you will want anything from a dozen to two dozen oysters, the larger number being better. Open the oysters, and strain their liquor over a quarter of a pound of stale breadcrumbs. When it is all absorbed, mash up the bread well with a fork. Mince the veal as finely as possible and add it to the soaked bread with a quarter of a pound of finely chopped suet, and salt and pepper to taste. Mix well, and then add the oysters cut up in small pieces and beaten with an egg. Pound all this well together, and either press into skins or make into small sausage shapes, and, after flouring them lightly, fry them in butter. Eat them hot or cold.

BOUILLABAISSE

It is really almost impossible to make Bouillabaisse in this country, but readers of my articles have so often asked for a recipe that I may perhaps give one here. This is strictly an English version! Enough for about six people. I have included it here because it is a great deal more than a soup : it is really more of a stew. Take a good-sized fresh haddock, three whiting, two small soles, one red mullet, one or two very small lobsters, and about a dozen mussels. (Cape lobster tails might be used instead of the lobster if expense must be considered.) Cut the fish into thick slices : the lobsters will have already been cooked. Now cut an onion and the white part of a large leek into thin rings. Put half a tumblerful of the best olive-oil you can get into a saucepan on a brisk fire, and, as soon as it is hot, put in the onions and leek. After four minutes put in all the fish except the lobsters, and sprinkle over a teaspoonful of potato flour, salt, pepper, and half a teaspoonful of curry powder. Toss the fish about in this for a few minutes, then add the lobsters cut in pieces, shell and all, two tomatoes chopped up without skin or pips, a tumblerful of dry white wine, and enough hot water to cover the whole. Finally add a little muslin bag containing a peeled clove of garlic, a quarter of a bayleaf, two slices of lemon without skin or pips, and a little piece of orange peel. Boil the whole thing very quickly for a quarter of an hour, and it is done. Take out the muslin bag, add a large pinch of very finely chopped parsley, and boil for half a minute. Dish the pieces of fish separately from the soup, but serve them to the guests together. The important things to remember are : the fish must be fresh ; the olive-oil must be good ; the boiling must be very rapid so that the oil will mix with the other liquid.

SOLE AU VIN BLANC

A common dish at restaurants, but not so common in cookery books. Butter a fireproof dish, and arrange in it four or five thin rounds of onion. Put on this bed your lightly salted sole, skinned side downwards. Add three-quarters of a glass of dry white wine, bring to the boil on the top of the fire, remove to the oven, and keep the liquid just on the move for about ten minutes, having put a piece of buttered paper over the dish. Meanwhile make a *roux* with butter and flour, moisten it with the strained cooking liquor from the sole, bind, off the fire, with two egg-yolks beaten in a little cream, and finish with a piece of butter in small bits. Disembarrass the sole of the onion rings, dish it up, and pour the sauce over it. If you like to brown it very quickly and lightly under the grill, do so. .

RABBIT A LA CRÈME

For this delicious dish you want a young rabbit weighing about a pound and a half when cut up for cooking. Heat a couple of ounces of butter in a pan, and, when it is hot, put in the pieces of rabbit and two ounces of onion cut in thick rounds. Fry until the meat is nicely coloured all over, then add three-quarters of a pint of stock, a table-spoonful of tomato purée, and salt and pepper. There ought to be just enough liquid to cover the pieces of rabbit. Now bring the sauce to the boil, cover the pan, and let it simmer for an hour. Leave a tiny space between the cover and the pan, so that the steam can escape and the liquid reduce. Ten minutes before serving, mix carefully and by degrees a level tablespoonful of flour with nine or ten spoonfuls of thick fresh cream, then pour this over the rabbit, shaking the pan so as to mix it with the gravy.

171

Make it all very hot without letting it actually boil, and scrape off as much as you can of the juices of the rabbit which have caramelised on the bottom of the pan. See that the sauce is well seasoned, take out the pieces of rabbit, remove the bits of onion clinging to them, put them into a dish, and strain the sauce over them.

STUFFED RED OR GREEN PEPPERS

It is better to blanch the red or green peppers (pimentos or capsicums) for five minutes or so in boiling water, or to fry or grill them lightly, before stuffing them. In either case the stalk end must be cut off (after parboiling or frying) and the inside pips carefully scooped out. Then stuff the peppers with any kind of cooked rice mixture you like, adding to it, if you wish, the flesh of one or two parboiled peppers. Make a sauce with stock and tomato purée, and in this bake the peppers for about fifteen minutes in a moderate oven.

RABBIT WITH TARRAGON

It might be well suspected that, as tarragon goes so well with chicken, it would do the same with rabbit. See that the rabbit is a young one. Season it with salt and pepper (having trussed it for roasting), stuff it with a mixture of breadcrumbs, chopped tarragon, and its own liver, and tie it over with fat bacon rashers. Roast it carefully, and, when it is half done, take out two or three tablespoonfuls of the dripping in the pan and put them into a small saucepan with the juice of half a lemon, salt, pepper, and a tablespoonful of chopped tarragon. Let this sauce simmer while the cooking is completed, and when the rabbit is relieved of his bacon overcoat and dished, strain the sauce over him.

RABBIT SALAD

If you should have roast rabbit over, try this salad for luncheon. Cut the rabbit meat into small pieces, and cut up an equal quantity of cold boiled waxy potatoes in the same way. Now add two medium-sized tomatoes, without their skins or pips, also cut in small pieces, two hard-boiled eggs cut in rounds, a handful of watercress leaves, and a spoonful each of chopped chervil and tarragon. Dress with olive-oil, vinegar, salt and pepper, in the proportion of one spoonful of vinegar to four of oil. Mix well together, before serving in a surround of lettuce.

GRILLED TROTTERS

Pig's feet may sound decidedly plebeian, but prepared in this way they are nevertheless quite excellent. Cut the prepared trotters in half lengthwise and wrap up each half in a piece of cloth, twisting each end well and tying it. Then cook them for four or five hours in water with salt, peppercorns, allspice, a large bouquet of parsley, thyme, and bayleaf, as well as two or three cloves of garlic, unless this is anathema to you. When the trotters are done, take them out of the water, let them cool, and then unwrap them. Roll them in olive-oil, and then in breadcrumbs, and grill them quickly. A quarter of an hour should be enough for both sides.

BOILED PARTRIDGE

Some years ago I was roundly taken to task by a well-known epicure for recommending to him a boiled young partridge. Like him, I had scoffed at such a waste of a young bird, when first I heard of it, but (as he was forced to do after tasting it) I remained to bless the inventor of so exquisite a dish. Indeed, I am not sure whether in this way you do not get the very finest flavour of the bird. Salt the bird inside and out, wrap it in vine leaves, and then in thin rashers of fat bacon, and boil it for thirty-five minutes in plain water, putting it in, of course, when the water is boiling. You must then immediately plunge it into iced water, and as soon as it is cold, take it out. The wrappings must be removed when it is served, and you will want no more with it than a delicately dressed lettuce.

BAKED SAUSAGES

Experimenting one day with a Chicken à la Maryland (which we have discussed on a previous page), we found that the chicken was a little too small, and not enough to feed some unexpected guests. Recourse was had to some chipolata sausages, and the discovery was made how good they can be when roasted in this way. Simply roll them in an egg beaten up with a tablespoonful of water, then breadcrumb them, and bake them in the oven, basting them well with butter, until they are a nice golden brown. Large sausages would be just as good this way, only they would, of course, take longer. They look so much more appetising than fried ones, and certainly taste far nicer.

RED CABBAGE A LA LIMOUSINE

This is a particularly good dish, and a great revelation to those who never think of red cabbage as anything but a pink and rather unpleasing pickle. Slice the cabbage finely, removing any hard stalky pieces, and let it soak in cold water for half an hour. Now put a piece of butter into a stewpan and a tablespoonful of stock, and the cabbage, put on the lid, and let it cook for three-quarters of an hour. Then add a few pieces of uncooked peeled chestnuts and some little bits of roast pork fat, put on the lid again, and finish cooking all together.

RED CABBAGE A LA POLONAISE

But if you haven't got pork fat or chestnuts, try this very savoury way. Having cut up the cabbage and soaked it, put it into a stewpan in handfuls straight out of the water, add a sour apple, peeled, cored, and sliced, an ounce of butter, a tablespoonful of chopped onion, a saltspoonful of salt, a little cayenne pepper, and a dash of grated nutmeg. Cook with the lid on (do not add any liquid at all) for an hour, then stir in a dessertspoonful of brown sugar and a tablespoonful of vinegar. Add also a pinch of powdered cloves and of cinnamon. Cook together for another five minutes, and serve very hot. It goes very well indeed with pork, especially a stewed knuckle.

MUSHROOMS

There are so many ways of cooking and serving mushrooms that perhaps I may be forgiven for recommending the very simplest. And that is to gather smallish ones, wipe them very carefully and do not peel them, cut off the stalks level with the heads, and put them, rounded side downwards, in a fireproof glass dish, so that each lies on the bottom (they must not be heaped up on each other). Put on the lid, and let them cook very slowly indeed in the oven. The exact time will depend on their size, but they should not take less than half an hour. An experiment in this direction will be found well worth while. Even cultivated mushrooms have been known to taste almost like wild ones when cooked in this way; but the cultivated ones must be peeled. Readers who possess an " Aga " Cooker will find that they take about an hour in the slow oven.

POTATO CAKES

The following recipes can be used either for deep or shallow frying. Either shape the mixture into small cakes or balls and fry in deep fat, or use a frying-pan and some butter to cook one large cake. The basis of each is ordinary mashed potato.

1. Add to the potato any sort of minced cold meat you have at hand and flavour it with onion, shallot, and a sprig or two of parsley all finely chopped.

2. Add flaked smoked haddock, moistening with milk, and seasoning with paprika pepper or a touch of curry powder.

3. Flaked salt cod is better than smoked haddock.

4. Add a finely chopped hard-boiled egg and a couple of minced anchovy fillets to each pound of potato.

5. Add, for each pound of potato, two slices of cooked lean ham, pounded up with fillet of herring in oil.

6. Add finely chopped lean ham ; brush egg over the cakes, and roll them in crushed vermicelli instead of breadcrumbs. Fry these only in deep fat.

BEETROOT

Beetroot can sometimes be overwhelmingly prolific. Here are three tips for using up an embarrassingly large crop.

Beetroot Salad. Cold beetroot swimming in vinegar can be

bettered a good deal if it is dressed in this way instead. Add to your beetroot slices a little very finely minced onion or tiny thinnest rings of it, and use the following sauce to dress it. Take three tablespoonfuls of made mustard, season them with salt and pepper and a few drops of lemon juice. Mix well together, and add gradually, stirring all the time, as much cream as you like.

Fried Beetroot. Cut a cooked beetroot into long slices and dip them into a batter made with a beaten egg, salt, pepper, a tablespoonful of flour, and a tablespoonful of white wine. Then roll them in a mixture of breadcrumbs and chopped parsley, and fry them carefully in deep fat.

Beetroot and Onion Pickle. Boil and slice the beetroots, and peel and slice some Spanish onions. Put alternate layers of each in a large jar, and cover them with a quart of vinegar which has been boiled with an ounce of mixed pepper, salt, and half an ounce of green ginger, and then allowed to get cold.

ORANGE ROLY-POLY

Make a light suet crust with half a pound of finely chopped suet, three-quarters of a pound of flour sieved with a tea-spoonful of baking powder and a pinch of salt, and enough water to make a fairly stiff paste. Roll out thinly, and put on it a layer of raw orange slices cut without skin, pith or pips. Sprinkle these with fine white breadcrumbs and brown sugar, wet the end of the paste or roll it up. Boil for about three hours in a floured cloth, and, when it is turned out, serve hot marmalade with it.

MILANESE FRITTERS

Boil up half a pint of milk with an ounce of lump sugar and half a vanilla-pod. While it is boiling, shower in a couple of ounces of semolina, keep stirring for a few minutes, then add half an ounce of unsalted butter, and cook slowly for twenty minutes. Remove the vanilla-pod (or if you have not used a vanilla-pod in the first instance, add a few drops of vanilla essence now), and stir in an ounce of chopped blanched almonds, the finely grated rind of half a lemon, and two beaten egg-yolks. Spread it out in a buttered tin to cool, and, when it is cold, cut it into rings from two to two-and-a-half inches in diameter, and brush them over with apricot jam diluted with a little Maraschino. Dip them in frying-batter, fry them in deep fat, and, when they are done, drain them, sprinkle them with icing-sugar, and serve them with a hot chocolate sauce handed separately.

NORMANDY PUDDING

Chop up, fairly coarsely, half a dozen peeled and cored cooking apples, and stir them up in a bowl with six ounces of breadcrumbs, a pinch of salt, a teaspoonful of cinnamon, and four ounces of castor sugar. Add gradually four beaten eggs, and, when all are well mixed, stir in the juice and grated rind of a lemon and a glass of rum or brandy. (The spirits can be omitted, if desired.) Put into a well-buttered mould or basin, cover with buttered paper and a cloth, and steam for about two hours. Serve a wine sauce with it.

CHEESE PUDDING

Grate three ounces of fine white breadcrumbs and put them in a basin. Boil half a pint of milk with an ounce of butter and pour it over the crumbs. Season with salt and pepper, a spot of cayenne, and a quarter of a teaspoonful of dry mustard. Then add the yolk of an egg and two ounces of grated cheese, and, when all is mixed together, finish by adding the well whisked white. Pour into a buttered pie-dish or shallow soufflé-dish, and bake until it is brown. Some might like even to add a few drops of onion juice, or to rub the dish round with garlic or onion, but it is excellent as it is, especially when made with Cheshire cheese.

HERRINGS' ROES WITH EGGS

Poach a few soft roes in milk, and season them with salt, cayenne pepper, and lemon juice. Now scramble as much egg as you want, add to it some finely chopped capers and a good deal of salt and pepper. Put some of this on narrow slices of buttered toast and lay a roe or two on top. Serve quickly and very hot.

HERRING'S ROE FINGERS

Bake some strips of puff pastry (or cheese pastry, if you like) about three inches by an inch and a half. On each quickly lay a soft herring's roe poached in milk and sprinkled with paprika pepper.

EPICURE'S TOASTS

Make some toast, butter it lightly when it is cold, and spread each piece with a mixture of Roquefort cheese, butter, and chopped dried walnuts in equal parts. Cold, of course.

NOVEMBER

THE KITCHEN GARDEN IN
NOVEMBER

PLENTY of digging work to be done, and the garden
roughed up. There is not a great deal of other
work that requires attention save that a careful look-
out must be kept on frosty nights, and adequate
protection be at hand. Protect *Globe Artichokes* from
the hard weather, and dig *Jerusalem Artichokes* when
wanted. It is a good idea to store a few of the latter
in case they are wanted when the ground is too hard
to dig. The *Asparagus* bed can now be cleaned up and
manured with dung or seaweed, and *Horseradish* can

181

be dug and stored. Last month *Rhubarb* should have been lifted for forcing, and this month the same must be done to *Seakale*. Sow a few rows of *Broad Beans*, if your soil is suitable : they should be up by Christmas Day, and make a pleasant omen for the new year. If you have the right sort of garden, a sowing of *Peas* may be made now, but, save in exceptional circumstances, my experience is that it is a very tricky business, to be regarded more as an experiment than anything else. A few *Carrots* can be sown in frames, if liked.

NOTES

NOVEMBER DISHES

FISH SOUP

Most fish can be used for this soup, but whiting would be a good one. Cook them in a *court-bouillon* flavoured rather mildly with vinegar, allowing a quart of this for each pound of fish. (A recipe for *court-bouillon* will be found under that for Grey Mullet on p. **60**.) Put the fish in the cold *court-bouillon*, bring it to the boil, and let it simmer gently until it is tender. Then take it out, remove the skin and bones, and rub the flesh through a fine sieve. Meanwhile boil the liquid quickly until it reduces to the quantity you want, strain it very carefully, rinse the saucepan, and put the liquid back with the sieved fish. Get it very hot without actually boiling it, and stir in a couple of egg-yolks beaten in a spoonful or two of cream. Finish with a few little bits of butter, after seasoning as you wish.

WATERCRESS SOUP

Pick off the leaves from a small bunch of watercress, and wash them well. Put them into a saucepan with a good piece of butter (the size of a small egg) and let them melt slowly. Now add about three-quarters of a pint of hot water, and two largish potatoes, peeled and cut in thin slices. Put on the lid, and boil quickly for half an hour. Rub the whole through a sieve, put the purée back on the fire, and add two cupfuls of boiled milk. Bring to the boil for a moment, season it, and the soup is ready. Bind with an egg-yolk beaten in a spoonful of milk or cream, if you like.

PEASANT SOUP

Slice up two carrots, two onions, two tomatoes, two leeks, two potatoes, and a small turnip, and let them stew for a while in a little butter. Now add a few sprigs of parsley, a clove, a few peppercorns, salt, and enough hot water to make the quantity of soup you want after allowing for reduction. Boil for about an hour, and rub the whole thing through a sieve. Now serve it as it is or bind it with a spoonful or two of cream and, if you like, an egg-yolk or two as well. But do not use stock in making this very simple soup. The plain water brings out all the simple flavours of the vegetables, and very delicious they are.

HOLLENDEN HALIBUT

One of the really good and simple American dishes. Put half a dozen thin slices of blanched pickled pork in a fireproof dish, spread some thinly sliced onion over them, and add a piece of bayleaf. On this bed lay a slice of halibut weighing about two pounds, and spread over it three full tablespoonfuls of butter kneaded with an equal quantity of flour. Sprinkle with buttered breadcrumbs, and arrange a few narrow strips of the pork on top. Cover with buttered paper, and bake for thirty-five minutes in a moderate oven. Then take off the paper, and bake for another quarter of an hour. Garnish with lemon, chopped parsley, and paprika, and serve with white sauce made with the cooking liquor instead of butter.

CURRIED PRAWNS

Curries, even when quite simply made, can be very delightful, and this one (which could equally well be applied to hard-boiled eggs, or lobster, or, say, haricot beans or lentils) is very easy ; so easy that it might very well be used in case of emergency. Fry a couple of small onions finely sliced in two ounces of butter, adding (if you will take my advice) a clove or half a clove of garlic. Stir in a tablespoonful of curry powder, and season with salt. Now add half a pound of peeled and quartered tomatoes, and a little water, enough to make a thickish sauce. Simmer this for a little, then put in the prawns, fresh or from a tin or glass, and let them cook very gently indeed for a quarter of an hour. Serve with very dry and hot plain boiled rice.

ROCK SALMON

There is something quite attractive about the texture and flavour of this fish (which a fishmonger tells me is nothing more than my old friend Ling), which we used to eat with gusto in Cornwall before the war. It lends itself to a savoury treatment, such as this very simple one. Have the fish divided into cutlets about an inch thick, season them well with salt and black pepper, and dredge them lightly with flour. Fry them golden on each side in a little butter. While they are frying, heat up some Escoffier Derby sauce, diluting it, if you like, with just a little water, and finishing it with a few small bits of butter. Cut up a few small gherkins in tiny strips and put them to warm with a few capers. Now criss-cross the rock salmon steaks with the gherkins, put a caper in each square, and serve with the sauce poured on and round them. A few plainly boiled potatoes cut to the shape of large olives would go well with this dish.

MEAT LOAF
Soak a dinner roll in milk, squeeze it as dry as you can, and put it through a mincing-machine with a pound of lean beef and the same of pork. Season with salt and plenty of pepper, and bind it with a beaten egg. Shape it into a loaf, brush over with white of egg, and sprinkle it with breadcrumbs. Now put it into a greased baking-tin, pour some boiling fat over it, and bake it in the oven, basting it alternately with its own fat and with sour cream. Use a cupful of the cream in all, and serve the basting mixture as a sauce when the loaf is browned.

PHEASANT A LA NORMANDE
You do not want your pheasant too well hung for this, and you must be able to eat all of it, because it is not nice when cold or made up after being cooked in this fashion. Brown the bird all over in butter, and while this is going on, cut half a dozen medium-sized apples in quarters, peel and core them, and mince them. Then toss them in butter and put a layer of them in the bottom of the pan in which the bird will be cooked, an earthenware terrine being the best, as then you can serve the pheasant in it. Lay the pheasant on the bed of apple, and put the rest round it. Pour over it a few spoonfuls of cream, put the lid on the terrine, and cook in the oven for half an hour or so. Guinea Fowl can be cooked very successfully in the same way.

SNIPE LOAF

Some time ago one of my readers in Burma sent me a recipe for a Snipe Loaf, which may well be welcome here. For it you will want a large white sandwich loaf. Scoop out the inside, leaving only the crust, and keep the top for a covering. Fry the whole thing crisp, including the top, in a frying-pan, and then fill up the inside with alternate layers of mushrooms, bacon, and snipe, the latter being cut in half and partly boned. When the loaf is nearly full, pour in a little brown sauce or gravy, cover with the top crust, and bake in a moderate oven for an hour to an hour and a half.

CHICKEN PIE

Cut the chicken up in convenient pieces, set them out on a dish, and sprinkle them with an ounce and a half of chopped mushrooms which have first been cooked in butter, the same quantity of finely chopped onions, and a pinch or two of freshly chopped parsley. On the bottom and sides of your pie-dish lay some thin slices of veal, and then arrange the pieces of chicken, seeing that the legs are at the bottom of the dish where they will cook better. Arrange here and there some thin pieces of bacon and two or three hard-boiled eggs cut in halves or quarters. Three-parts fill the dish with chicken consommé or chicken stock, made so that it will form a fine jelly if you want to eat the pie cold, cover with a layer of puff paste, and bake in a moderate oven for an hour and a half. Pour some more stock in through the slit when it is done. You will probably find that a rather pronounced flavour of tarragon in the stock will be an advantage, but the flavour of the pie will, of course, depend to a very great extent on the flavour of the stock.

SAUCISSES GRATINÉES

This is just a slightly different way of serving sausages. Fry your sausages, and lean them elegantly round a heap of mashed potato in your serving dish. Sprinkle the whole thing over with a half-and-half mixture of breadcrumbs and grated cheese, pour over it a little of the fat from the sausage frying, and brown it for five or six minutes in a hot oven.

PARTRIDGE A LA LAUTREC

Cut down the back of the young partridge, flatten it slightly, and skewer it. Season it with salt and pepper, sprinkle it with melted butter, and grill it gently. Dish it with a few mushrooms on each side. These have been grilled, too, and each is garnished with a small spoonful of maître d'hôtel butter. Sprinkle the partridge last of all with a few drops of lemon juice, and, if you like, surround each mushroom with a thread of melted meat glaze.

RABBIT A L'ESTOUFFADE

Salt and pepper some little *lardons* of fat bacon and use them to lard a rabbit trussed for roasting. After you have then lightly browned the rabbit all over in butter put it in a stewpan or casserole, the bottom of which you have lined with rashers of bacon or pickled pork. Add a tea-cupful of stock and a glass of Madeira. Put in as well fifteen or so button onions, half a dozen small carrots cut in four lengthwise, a bouquet of three or four parsley stalks, a quarter of a bayleaf and a tiny sprig of thyme, and a fair sprinkling of salt. Close the pan as tightly as you can, fixing the lid on with a paste of flour and water, if you like, and cook on a low heat, very gently, for an hour or an hour and a half according to the age of the rabbit. Serve it on a dish, straining the sauce over it at the last minute.

SALADE LORETTE

I have already mentioned Corn Salad, otherwise Lamb's Lettuce, otherwise *Mâche*, otherwise *Doucette*, and a delicious salading it is. It is the basis of the well-known *Salade Lorette*, which is made in this way. Cut a beetroot and a head of celery into dice, and prepare the Corn Salad by washing it and drying it well. For each person allow a handful of the leaves and a tablespoonful each of beetroot and celery. Mix all together in a salad-bowl with a plain

189

French dressing, two parts olive-oil, one part wine vinegar, salt and pepper. Mix carefully again after the dressing has been finished, but see that you do not bruise the corn salad leaves.

ONION RAGOUT

An excellent dish, given me by a friend who used to live in Smyrna. It is very good with dishes of lamb or mutton. Put two pounds of small onions into a stewpan with two ounces of butter, and fry them a golden brown. Then add two tablespoonfuls of white wine, a few cloves, a small stick of cinnamon, and two bayleaves. Moisten with half a pint of good stock, and add half a pound of tomatoes rubbed through a fine sieve. Simmer all together for about an hour, or until the onions are tender, and serve hot.

CHESTNUT CROQUETTES

Boil some chestnuts, mash them, and take a breakfast-cupful of the purée. Mix this with some very finely minced onions, which have been stewed in a little butter (or simply with some onion salt), season with celery salt and pepper, and bind with a couple of egg-yolks beaten up with two tablespoonfuls of cream. Shape the mixture into croquettes, egg-and-breadcrumb them, and fry them in deep fat. Good with roast pheasant or hare.

WATERCRESS PURÉE

As an accompaniment, for example, to grilled lamb cutlets, this beats spinach to a frazzle ! But it is not very cheap. For four or five people you will want a pound and a half, which you must pick over, removing dead leaves, thick stalks, and the various foreign bodies which it seems to attract. Wash the leaves very well, and cook them in plenty of boiling salted water without a lid. Keep boiling hard for a quarter of an hour, then put them in a colander and plunge this at once into cold water. Drain them as well as you can, pressing them between your hands to extract as much moisture as possible, then put them on a board and chop them finely. Now put them into a wide pan with two "nuts" of butter—that is, about two ounces altogether—and stir on a quick fire for five minutes so that the last trace of unnecessary moisture evaporates. Then season with salt and pepper, sprinkle with a dessertspoonful of flour, mix well, and then add three good spoonfuls of stock or milk. Stir on until it boils, then cover, and let it simmer gently for twenty minutes to half an hour. Stir in a few small bits of butter before serving this very delicious and beautifully coloured dish.

POTATO STICKS

Bake some potatoes in the oven, sieve them, and weigh out five ounces of the purée. Mix this well with three and a half ounces of butter, the same of flour, a yolk of egg, and a pinch of salt. Roll out this paste and cut it into strips three inches long and an inch wide. Brush them with beaten egg, sprinkle them with a little more salt, and bake them in a very hot oven until golden. A little cheese could be added in the mixing if liked.

ARTICHOKE CHIPS

Jerusalem artichokes make excellent fried chips for serving with grills. They should be treated in exactly the same way as potatoes.

ARTICHOKE FRITTERS

A useful dish as a vegetable or savoury course. Cook a pound of Jerusalem artichokes in milk, not too well done, and cut them in slices. Sprinkle them with oil, vinegar, salt, and pepper, and leave them for half an hour. Then drain them and dry them, sprinkle them with a little freshly grated cheese, dip them in fritter batter, and fry them golden in hot fat.

APRICOT PURÉE

Make a good hot apricot purée, and use it to pour over a nice amount of small, crustless dice of stale bread fried in butter, the bread being about half an inch thick. While you are frying the bread dice, make a thick syrup by boiling a glass of sweet Madeira with twice the amount of sugar, and use this to pour over the purée. It should be eaten at once.

PINEAPPLE IN MELON

Peel an oblong green or yellow melon, cut it in half lengthwise, take out the seeds, put the halves together again, and soak them for a couple of hours in some hot syrup flavoured with ginger. When it is cold, drain it, and stuff it with a mixture of stiffly whipped cream and cubes of pineapple. Serve as cold as possible, and use fresh pineapple if you can. If not, I find the tinned Hawaiian ones are the best.

SUNDAY PUDDING

A very old friend gave me this recipe for what is a kind of innocuous Christmas pudding, but really very light and pleasant. Part of its beauty lies in the naïve title of the recipe that follows it. Take half a pint of raisins, half a pound of currants, half a pound each of suet and bread-crumbs, a tablespoonful of flour, half a glassful of brandy, a small piece of grated lemon peel, three ounces of brown sugar, a teacupful of milk, and four eggs. Mix these all well together, put them into a greased pudding-basin, and steam for four hours. If there is any over, try the next dish.

MONDAY PUDDING

Put some slices of cold Sunday pudding in the bottom of a mould. Make a custard by bringing slowly to the boil half a pint of full milk, a small piece of cinnamon, a fingernail of lemon peel, and a bayleaf. When it has boiled and cooled, add the yolks of four eggs. Beat well, and strain it over the slices of pudding in the basin, and put this into a pan of water and steam it for an hour. A custard sauce would be very good with both these sweets.

DUCHY TOASTS

Fry a few minced mushrooms in a little butter until they are almost a purée, and season them with salt and pepper. Have ready some toasts surmounted by a piece of grilled

192

streaky bacon, and spread this with some of the mushroom purée. Finish with a spoonful of scrambled egg, and, if you can manage it, with a small grilled mushroom on top of all.

FRIED SARDINES

Drain, wipe, and skin and bone some good sardines, brush them over with a little thin mustard, sprinkle them with a few drops of lemon juice, egg-and-breadcrumb them, and fry them in deep fat. Serve very hot and well drained.

DECEMBER

THE KITCHEN GARDEN IN
DECEMBER

EVERYTHING is more or less quiescent, and a good
deal of the gardener's task consists of. chopping
and sawing wood ! But he will find all sorts of odd
jobs to do, from tidying up and " improving " to getting ready for the growing season. It is a good idea
to earth up the *Broad Beans* when they appear, and
no harm is done by earthing up the grown greenstuff
in windy places. Blanch *Endive*, and see that your
Parsley plants are protected. A cloche put over roots
of *Mint* and *Tarragon* will ensure earlier supplies than

usual in the spring. *Corn Salad* may be covered with the cloches, too, and a supply kept up along with the covered *Lettuces*.

NOTES

CARROT AND TOMATO SOUP

Take twice as many carrots as tomatoes. Slice the carrots and stew them in butter with a slice of onion, a piece of celery, a sprig of parsley, and a bacon bone. Add the tomatoes cut in quarters, a teaspoonful of sugar, and the same of cream of tartar. Moisten with the necessary quantity of stock, and when the carrots are quite done, take out the bacon bone and the parsley, and pass the rest through a sieve. Enrich, if you wish, with a little cream, and serve with croûtons of fried bread.

POTAGE LIVONIEN

Cut in thin strips some carrots, turnip, celery, leeks, onions, and add a little chopped parsley. Cook all these together in salted water for half an hour. Then drain them, and stew them for a few minutes in butter, adding two table-spoonfuls of cooked rice. Cover with stock or water, and cook on until the vegetables are quite done. Rub all through a sieve, season with salt and a pinch of sugar, and stir in a cupful of cream. Heat through, bind, if you like, with egg-yolk, and serve with fried croûtons.

LOBSTER CHOWDER

Cut up in dice two pounds of cooked lobster meat, and cream two tablespoonfuls of butter, mixing them with the green part from the lobster and a couple of tablespoonfuls of finely crushed water biscuit. Put a slice of onion in a pint of cold milk, bring it slowly to the boil, and then strain it on to the butter and lobster mixture. Meanwhile cover the lobster shell with cold water, bring it to the boil, and boil for ten minutes. Strain this liquor, add to it the milk, etc., put in the lobster meat, season with salt and paprika pepper, heat well through, and serve.

EGGS WITH SWEET CORN

Make a creamy purée with a tin of sweet corn, and arrange on it your eggs, which will look best if they are poached, but if you prefer it they could be hard-boiled. Sprinkle them with very fine strips of cold, lean, cooked ham and of pimentos (sweet peppers, which you can get cheaply in tins), and cover all with white meat jelly made from chicken stock and veal bones.

EGGS IN JELLY

For these you will want some really good consommé made in such a way that it will set to a light jelly. As a matter of fact (although I am no advocate for tinned foodstuff as a rule, and especially in the country where the empty tins are a real problem) a tin of Heinz's Chicken Consommé would do admirably. Poach the eggs, trim them neatly, and put them in a dish, or in small dishes one in each. Decorate round them with little pieces of vegetable—carrots, a few peas perhaps, a little heap of asparagus tips—and then cover them with the warm jelly, which must not be hotter than just enough to melt it. If the garnishes round the outside are light and likely to float, like peas, it is best to put just a thin layer of jelly round the egg first, and then let the vegetables stick to it before you fill up the dish enough to cover the egg. They make a pleasant first course for luncheon, and are very useful as a stand-by for unexpected guests.

OMELETTE BOULONNAISE

Poach some soft herrings' roes and use them to stuff a plain omelette, mixing them with a little maître d'hôtel butter. When the omelette is stuffed and dished, pour a little of the same butter melted round it.

A DISH OF COD

Take two pounds of the tail-end of cod and make a few scores on each side of it. Marinate it for an hour, turning it over five or six times, in a glassful of dry white wine, three tablespoonfuls of olive-oil, salt, pepper, a medium-sized carrot, onion and a shallot all minced finely, and three or four parsley stalks, a sprig of thyme and half a bayleaf. When the hour is up, wipe the fish, and put it in a thickly buttered fireproof dish. Strain the marinade through a fine strainer, and pour it round the fish. Bring it to the boil on top of the stove, and brush the fish over with melted butter. Cook it in a hot oven for half an hour or so, basting it now and then with the liquor. About seven minutes before it is ready, sprinkle the top of the fish with breadcrumbs. At the last minute, squeeze a quarter of a lemon over it. Serve with boiled potatoes sprinkled with parsley and melted butter.

SCALLOPS EN COQUILLE

This is a very savoury way of cooking scallops in their shells. Put them in cold water, bring to the boil, and poach them for five minutes. Take them out, drain them, and cut them up small. Mix them with the flesh of a skinned tomato in little bits, a very small onion, some parsley, and three or four mushrooms finely chopped together. Cook these all together in butter for a few minutes, season them, and then bind them with a little thick Béchamel or white sauce. Put this mixture into the shells, and after sprinkling them either with a little cream or with fine breadcrumbs, brown them in the oven. The main thing is to see that the flavour of the vegetables is not too overpowering, or the delicacy of the scallops will be lost.

A FISH PIE

Some years ago a friend sent me a private cookery book from France, and among the many attractive recipes in it was this one for a Fish Pie.

Boil and divide into large flakes some cod, and parboil about the same amount of potatoes. Cut these in slices, and in a rather deep fireproof dish put layers of potato, cod, white sauce, and grated cheese until the dish is full. Let the last two layers be potato and the sauce. Now sprinkle it well with grated cheese and breadcrumbs, and cook in the oven until the top is nicely browned.

BRAIN FRITTERS

After soaking the brains well to remove all trace of blood, put them in a saucepan well covered with cold water, and add a few slices of onion, a bouquet of parsley, thyme, and bayleaf, a clove, salt, a few peppercorns, and three or four spoonfuls of wine vinegar. Bring to the boil and let them poach gently for twenty-five minutes. Now let them get cold between two plates, with a weight on the top one. Then cut them in small slices, and let them marinate for half an hour in a mixture of lemon juice, salt, pepper, chopped parsley, and a few drops of olive-oil. Then drain and dry them, dip them in fritter batter, and fry them in deep fat.

TRIPES A LA DAUPHINOISE

This demands a bottle of wine and a little brandy, but the tripe is cheap enough, and the dish is excellent for a cold day. Melt a good spoonful of butter in an earthenware cocotte or casserole, and put into it a turnip, two onions, and two carrots, all cut in rounds, a bouquet of parsley, tarragon, celery, and thyme, a clove of garlic, several bits of bacon rind tied together and a couple of pounds of dressed tripe cut in small squares. Put the pan on a quick fire, so as to colour the contents slightly, then pour in three-quarters of a pint of dry white wine and the same quantity of stock. Season with salt, pepper, two cloves, and a pinch of nutmeg. Bring to the boil, cover the pan as closely as possible, and cook in a slow oven for three hours. Just before serving, take out the bouquet, the garlic, and the bacon rinds, and pour in a small glassful of burnt brandy. Serve and eat very hot.

MILANESE CUTLETS

Trim the lamb cutlets nicely, and dip them in melted butter. Now cover them with a half-and-half mixture of grated Parmesan cheese and breadcrumbs. Shake off what loose crumbs there are, and dip the cutlets very carefully in beaten egg. Cover them again with the cheese and breadcrumb mixture, dip them finally in melted butter, and then grill them gently and slowly. Serve them with a tomato sauce.

TURKEY

The Christmas aftermath always leaves us with turkey

scraps, and the disposal of the last of these in a fashion approved by the economically-minded is an anxious question. My own solution is pancakes. Cut the turkey remains into very small pieces, and bind them with any sort of sauce you care to make, preferably a well flavoured white one. Add, if you like, a few chopped tinned mushrooms, though this is by no means essential. Have the mixture warm and ready while you make a number of very thin and small pancakes with unsweetened batter. In each of these roll up some of the turkey, arrange them when stuffed on a long dish, pour a little of your sauce over them, sprinkle them with grated cheese, and brown very quickly.

BEEF CAKES

Sometimes it is the very simple dish that appears to be the most exquisite, and in this dish of beef you certainly get the full flavour of the meat. Get the butcher to mince you freshly (or, better, have it done in your own kitchen) some good beef, rump steak being a good cut for this. Put it into a basin, season it well with salt and pepper, and then bind it with egg-yolk, two egg-yolks to a pound of the mince being about enough. Now shape the mixture into little balls and flatten them out to cakes about an inch thick and from two to three inches in diameter. Melt some butter in a frying-pan, and fry the cakes quickly in this. They should be nicely browned outside but still pink inside. Drain them on kitchen paper, and pour into the pan a small cupful of cream with a teaspoonful of French mustard diluted with enough warm water to melt it. Stir well, and scrape the juices from the bottom of the pan, and let the cream boil a little and thicken. It will make a fine dark coffee-coloured sauce, which you must pour round the beef cakes on serving them. You may want to add a little more salt and pepper to the sauce before it is quite to your taste.

LAMB CUTLETS SOUBISE

Trim the cutlets, and cook them lightly on one side only.

Then let them get cold pressed between two plates. Meanwhile you will have made some good onion sauce without lumps, and some white sauce, too. Mix these in equal proportions, and, when the mixture is cold, spread it thickly over the cooked side of each cutlet. Then egg-and-breadcrumb them, and cook them in the oven, basting them with butter.

POTATO PANCAKES

Make an ordinary pancake batter, adding a little salt to it, and, when it has waited the proper time, mix it smoothly with about a third of its volume of finely mashed potato. Make the mixture into pancakes in the usual way, and serve them with melted butter.

SCOTS POTATOES

Parboil some potatoes and cut them in rounds about an eighth of an inch thick. Dip these in a mixture of two eggs beaten up with a tablespoonful of fine breadcrumbs and the same of grated, lean, cooked ham or bacon, and fry them in deep fat.

STUFFED TOMATOES

Roast, peel, and skin some chestnuts, about three for each tomato. Chop up a shallot or a small onion, and cook it in butter without browning it. Add the chestnuts roughly chopped, season with salt, pepper, and a little lemon juice, and heat through. Scoop out the tomatoes and fill them with this mixture. Sprinkle with breadcrumbs, pour over a little melted butter, and bake in the oven for ten minutes or so. Of course, only the core and pips of the tomatoes should be taken out, leaving the flesh on the inside of the skins.

SALSIFY A LA NORMANDE

Boil the salsify in the usual way, but instead of serving it with a white sauce use the following Sauce Normande. Melt a large nut of butter over a gentle flame, and in it lightly brown an onion chopped very finely. Add another piece of butter and a tablespoonful of flour, and let them cook a little together. Moisten with cider, stirring well and adding some more tiny pieces of butter. Season with salt, pepper, and a little grated nutmeg or cinnamon, and, just before serving, whip in some fresh cream with a squeeze of lemon juice at the very last.

This sauce, by the way, is an excellent one for other vegetables, too, such as cauliflower, asparagus, carrots or leeks.

ENDIVES A LA FLAMANDE

In France what we call chicory is known as endive, so that this dish must be made with those long white objects which the greengrocer will sell you under the name of chicory. Prepare two pounds of them by removing discoloured leaves and cutting the hard part of the root off, and cut the vegetables across in rounds about the thickness of your finger. Wash them, and dry them in a cloth. Now butter the bottom and sides of a stewpan or casserole just large enough to hold them when they are well pressed down, put the rounds into it, put a circle of buttered paper on top of them, cover tightly, and cook in a slow oven for at least two hours. By then all the liquid from the endives should have evaporated, so that you should now be able to turn them out like a cake, quite compact and slightly browned. Just sprinkle this with salt, and serve it.

ALMOND PASTE WITH APPLES

Almond paste as a filling for baked apples may sound unusual, but it is good. Make your almond paste in the usual way, and having peeled and cored as many apples as you want, fill them with the paste, and bake them.

HARD SAUCE

The best sauce for Christmas pudding by a long chalk. Cream four good tablespoonfuls of butter, gradually add two level tablespoonfuls of castor sugar until the mixture is light and frothy. Then add a suspicion of nutmeg and either half a teaspoonful of vanilla essence or lemon juice, or a tablespoonful of brandy or rum. Keep it on ice or in a cold place to harden.

POTS DE CRÈME AU CHOCOLAT

Nearly fill eight little earthenware pots with milk (you can get the special little pots for this from Fortnum & Mason, but any little pot would do), and put this into a saucepan with three ounces of castor sugar and as much grated chocolate as you will want, about four ounces. (It depends on how strong you like the flavour of chocolate.) Boil it up, and let it get cold. Now beat up the yolks of six eggs (" potted " ones would do), add them to the milk, and pass the whole through a hair sieve. Fill the pots with this, and cook them in the oven in a dish of hot water, covering them with greased paper, until they are set. Observe the same precautions as you would if baking a custard. Alternatively they will cook admirably in a very slow oven. Coffee ones could be made by using a mixture of milk and very strong coffee, and in making either it is always a good thing to put in the chocolate ones just a slight flavour of coffee, and chocolate in the coffee ones.

AMERICAN PANCAKES

Having made your pancakes in the usual way, and kept them flat while keeping hot, have ready mixed two tablespoonfuls of fresh melted butter, a pinch of cinnamon, and three tablespoonfuls of dissolved red currant jelly. Spread one side of each pancake with some of this mixture, roll up, arrange them on a long dish, sprinkle them with icing sugar, and glaze them quickly.

CHEESE SAVOURY

Mix up in a basin some cream cheese with salt, pepper, finely minced onion, and paprika pepper. Add some finely chopped olives and a dash of cayenne. Spread this pleasant mixture on buttered bread or toast, and decorate with a small ring cut across a stuffed olive.

TOMATO RAREBIT

Make a white sauce with two tablespoonfuls of butter, the same of flour, and three-quarters of a breakfast-cupful of

thin cream or milk, seasoning it with salt. Put it into
a double saucepan, and add a little made mustard, three-
quarters of a breakfast-cupful of tomato rubbed through
a sieve, two cups of grated cheese, and two beaten eggs.
Stir and cook until thick, then serve on toasts.

A FEW RIVER FISH

A FEW RIVER FISH

MOST fishermen, I find, have very decided ideas about cooking the fish they catch, but there are occasionally times when an unusual recipe is sought or cook finds herself confronted by an unfamiliar catch without the master hand to guide her. It may be useful, therefore, for the hostess to be able to refer to a few recipes here that she might not find otherwise. They are for the most part French, for, with all due respect to our English cooking, river fish are much more pleasantly eaten over there, principally because there are more rivers, I suppose, and even in these days of modern transport the sea is so far from many parts of the country. The French are more economically minded than we are, too, so we can be grateful to them for teaching us once more a thing or two.

Before taking the fish in alphabetical order, let me give two recipes which are needed here, or rather let me repeat them, for they have been given before in the body of this book.

MATELOTE

All kinds of river fish can be used in this very savoury and pleasant dish, of which the Matelote of Eels is perhaps best known in this country. In the mixed one, eels, tench, pike, barbel, and so on can all be used together. Cut the prepared fish into pieces two or three inches long : there should be about two pounds altogether. Now in a shallow saucepan or frying-pan put your pieces of fish, four ounces of minced onion, a bouquet of parsley, thyme, and bay-leaf, a good pinch of salt, and a bottle of red wine (or white, if you would prefer it). Add also a small piece of garlic about the size of a haricot bean, crushed. Bring quickly to the boil, pour in a sherry-glassful of brandy, and set it alight. When it has burned out, put on the lid, and boil fairly quickly for a quarter of an hour. Then take out the pieces of fish and keep them warm. Strain the liquor into a basin, rinse the pan in hot water, and pour the liquor back again. Continue to boil it until you have reduced it by a third, then add a small spoonful of flour kneaded with two " nuts " of butter, and boil and stir for two minutes. Add pepper and a few button onions and mushrooms which you have already cooked in butter. Put back the pieces of fish, and simmer very quietly for five minutes. Arrange the pieces of fish in a dish, surround them with the onions and mushrooms, pour over the sauce (which you have finished with a few bits of butter), and finally set round half a dozen croûtons of fried bread.

In cooking river fish the French usually make use of a *Court-bouillon* with wine or vinegar. Here they are.

Court-bouillon with Vinegar. Cut up two medium carrots and two onions, and stew them in a little butter for five minutes. Add a bouquet of parsley, thyme, and bayleaf. Pour in your water, and for each pint add a tablespoonful of wine vinegar. Bring to the boil and simmer for an hour, adding a few peppercorns ten minutes before the stock is finished. Strain well, and let it get cold before using it.

Court-bouillon with White Wine. A pint and a half of white wine, a pint and a half of water, a medium-sized carrot and an onion, a bouquet of parsley, thyme, and bayleaf, a dessertspoonful of salt, four peppercorns. Cook as above.

Court-bouillon with Red Wine. Three pints of red wine, two carrots and two onions, a bouquet of parsley, thyme, and bayleaf, two shallots, one tablespoonful of salt, four peppercorns. Cook as above.

BARBEL

This is a way with barbel in Central France. After scaling, cleaning, and washing very well a barbel of about three pounds, marinate it for two hours in two spoonfuls of olive-oil and a small glass of brandy, turning it five or six times. Now take it out and cook it in a couple of pints of red wine with a clove of garlic, some onions, shallots, parsley and chives, and a seasoning of salt and pepper. By the time the fish is cooked the liquid ought to have reduced by three-quarters. While the fish has been cooking you will have fried a quarter of a pound of mushrooms in a quarter of a pound of butter, and to this you must now add two tablespoonfuls of cream. Strain the wine from the fish into this mixture, and cook it quietly for twenty minutes. Serve the barbel, covered with this delicious sauce.

BREAM

After washing, scaling, and cleaning the fish, score them in three or four places on each side, and let them lie for a good hour in a marinade of olive-oil, lemon juice, parsley, thyme, bayleaf, salt and pepper. Turn them over now and again. While they are marinating put a good glass of white wine in a pan, add a chopped shallot, put the pan on a strong heat, and let the wine reduce away practically altogether. Put the pan now on the side of the stove, add half a teaspoonful of made mustard, four ounces of butter, two hard-boiled egg-yolks pounded up, some chopped parsley, salt, and coarsely ground black pepper. Mix the sauce well and keep it hot, while you grill the bream quickly, basting them frequently with melted butter. When they are done, serve them with the sauce poured over them.

CARP

Carpe à l'alsacienne is a well-known and simple dish. Brown lightly two minced medium-sized onions in three dessertspoonfuls of olive-oil, add a minced shallot and a piece of garlic the size of a haricot bean, sprinkle with a dessertspoonful of flour, and let it brown lightly. Now moisten with about a pint of stock, add a bouquet of parsley, thyme, and bayleaf, and season with salt and a good deal of pepper. Put on the lid, and cook this gently for half an hour. Prepare a carp weighing a little over two pounds, putting aside the roe. Cut the fish across in slices, put it in the strained sauce you have just been cooking, and cook it hard for twenty minutes. Take out the pieces, drain them, and arrange them in a dish. Strain the sauce again, adding a spoonful of coarsely chopped parsley and chervil mixed, and pour this over the fish. Let it get cold before serving it. The sauce should set to a jelly. The roe should be put into the liquor just two minutes before the fish will have finished cooking.

Carp can be grilled, either whole or in slices. It should first be brushed over with olive-oil. It is then served on anchovy or some other butter, or on a purée of sorrel.

EEL A LA TARTARE

You will want an eel of about three-quarters of a pound, prepared and cut in pieces about three inches long. Put the pieces in a stewpan with a pint and a half of *court-bouillon* with white wine, warm. Bring to the boil and boil gently for twenty minutes. Let the pieces get cold in the liquor, then take them out, drain them, and dry them in a cloth. Now egg-and-breadcrumb them, grill them or fry them in deep fat, drain them, and serve them with a Tartare sauce.

Very small eels can be cleaned and skinned, beheaded, dipped in milk, then in flour, and fried, *à la meunière*, in a little butter. The butter, slightly browned and flavoured with chopped parsley and lemon juice, is poured over on serving.

GUDGEON

These little fish can be fried in a pleasantly decorative manner called, in French cooking, *en manchons*—that is, in muffs. Having cleaned them, dip them in milk, drain them, roll them in flour, then egg-and-breadcrumb them. Roll them in the palm of your hand to press the breadcrumbs well on to them, and take off with your fingers the breadcrumbs coating the head and tail, so that these are left bare again. They then look as if they are wearing a muff of egg-and-breadcrumbs. Fry them for four or five minutes in deep fat, and serve them surrounded by lemon and fried parsley.

PERCH

It is recommended that medium-sized perch should be cooked in a *court-bouillon* with vinegar, but using only half the quantity of the vinegar given in the foregoing recipe. They can also be scored on each side, and grilled and served with a hot Ravigote sauce made as follows. Make a white *roux* with a large nut of butter and a small spoonful of flour. Moisten it with half a pint of stock, and let it simmer gently. In another pan put four spoonfuls of wine vinegar, four spoonfuls of white wine, and a spoonful of chopped shallot, and let the wine and vinegar reduce to three spoonfuls in all. Add the sauce to this, and let it simmer for five minutes. Finally stir in, with the pan off the fire, two nuts of butter in small pieces and a spoonful of chives, chervil, and tarragon chopped and mixed together.

PIKE

There is a very large number of ways of cooking and serving pike on the Continent, and here is a good way of stuffing it. After having prepared the fish, salt it inside and out, and leave it for a few hours. Meanwhile make a stuffing with its liver and roe, a piece of breadcrumb the size of an egg soaked in gravy or stock, several mushrooms, two filleted anchovies, two ounces of butter, *fines herbes* (that is, parsley, chives, chervil, and tarragon), a beaten egg, and a good seasoning of salt and pepper. Stuff the pike with this, wrap it up in a double piece of buttered paper, twisting or tying up each end firmly, and cook the fish in the oven, serving it with a sauce according to your fancy.

If you get a good pike, it is excellent when plainly cooked in a *court-bouillon* with vinegar or white wine, and served with plain boiled potatoes and Hollandaise sauce.

TENCH

These are often fried, and for the best results should be split like a mackerel. Simply flour them, and fry them in deep fat.

TROUT AU BLEU

This restaurant dish is always amazing, but it can be done quite easily at home, if the trout stream is not far away. The fish should really be cooked immediately after they are killed if the best kind of desired blue colour is to be obtained. But quite good results can be got from fish that have not been killed very long. *Court-bouillon* with vinegar or with red wine is used. As soon as the fish are ready pour some boiling vinegar over them, then put them into a barely warm *court-bouillon*. After this comes to the boil, four or five minutes of poaching is enough. Serve them hot or cold, with melted butter or a mayonnaise or Tartare sauce. For correctness the trout should be tied, before cooking, with a piece of thread, the head to the tail.

HERBS IN THE KITCHEN

HERBS IN THE KITCHEN

FOR many years, the cultivation of herbs for cookery had fallen into general disuse, except for the flavouring of stuffings and in those national sauces, like mint sauce and parsley sauce, which, with onion sauce, have been declared to be our only efforts in this direction. Most people were satisfied (and still are, I fear) with a packet or bottle of " mixed herbs " ; and, provided they had a strong enough flavour to make themselves obvious, little attempt was made to differentiate between the various ingredients. It was unusual to find, in a kitchen garden, much more than a few clumps of parsley, mint, and sage ; and, as a well-known writer on food has complained, the parsley would have been better employed in the dish than garnishing it outside. The greater interest that has been taken in food and in cookery during the past few years has brought about a change, and I believe that people are now more interested in herbs than ever before. Although this interest has arisen out of cooking, a great many people are still ignorant of the particular uses of the various herbs. I would like, therefore, to give some idea here, with a few recipes, of ways in which different herbs can be used in the kitchen ; and, for a rough-and-ready method of assembling my notes, I will take the order in which these herbs are dealt with in the *Bulletin*.* I ought,

* *Bulletin on Herbs* (No. 76) issued by the Ministry of Agriculture (1*s*. nett), from which this chapter is reprinted.

perhaps, to add that while Continental nations have always treated herbs with greater respect and discrimination than we have, sweet herbs were, of course, very largely, and often indiscriminately, used in our kitchens in past centuries. Whether this was because the popular palate was less refined than it is nowadays, or, as has often been suggested, in order to disguise the inferior quality of the meat or fish, I cannot say ; but the fact remains that not only was the " bunch of sweet herbs " fairly omnipresent, but a great many herbs and seasonings were employed in cooking which would not be tolerated nowadays.

PARSLEY

While seedsmen have concentrated their efforts on producing a beautiful curled plant for decoration, oddly enough the principal use to which this herb can be put demands the stalk rather than the leaf. I mean the *Bouquet garni*, so much and so admirably used in French cooking for flavouring stock and various sauces. This bouquet (the classic bunch of sweet herbs, perhaps) which Escoffier rather bluntly and far less picturesquely calls a " faggot," consists of two or three parsley stalks, a sprig of thyme, and a bayleaf tied together. (If any of the constituents are dried, then the bouquet is enclosed in a little piece of butter muslin, the aim in either instance being that it can be taken out of the stock, etc., when necessary.) The bouquet is invariably put into stock at the same time as the vegetables, and accounts for a good deal of the savouriness of French soups and sauces. It is a practice highly to be recommended, and an increasing number of English cooks make use of this delicious addition, the presence of which is really a hall-mark of good cooking. The other principal uses of parsley are for making parsley sauce, fried parsley, and the usual veal forcemeat familiar to us all, also in maître d'hôtel butter, which consists of butter pounded up with very finely chopped parsley and a touch of lemon juice. This is used as a garnish for certain fried or grilled fish and with grilled meats.

MINT

Mint sauce has already been mentioned. English people are usually fond of vinegar, otherwise they would prefer mint jelly, which is really apple jelly flavoured with mint, mint leaves being infused in the apple juice before the sugar is added. In some French dishes, mint is included in the mixed herbs, but not in many. Its most famous use after mint sauce, is in the American Mint Julep, one of the recipes for which is as follows : Add the leaves from a bunch of fresh mint to a cupful of lemon juice and half a cupful of water, and stir in a cupful and a half of castor sugar. Leave for half an hour. Put a large piece of ice in a jug or bowl and pour this infusion over it, adding three pints of ginger ale. A good drink for hot weather.

SAGE

This very strong herb is, of course, best known in sage and onion stuffing, which it usually dominates to the exclusion of even the flavour of the meat it stuffs. I have found, however, that there is a faint affinity between dressed crab and sage, provided that the latter is used in infinitesimal quantities.

TARRAGON

Tarragon is one of the most delicate and delicious of all the herbs, and it is a pity that it is not better known ; it is often difficult to obtain it fresh. Tarragon vinegar is fairly popular among those who exercise discrimination in salad dressing, and is quite easy to make at home. All that is necessary is to steep some fresh tarragon leaves in white wine vinegar (a teacupful to a quart of vinegar) in a closed jar for six weeks, and then to strain off and bottle the impregnated liquid. Tarragon has a perfect affinity with chicken, and to a lesser degree with rabbit, the addition of a few leaves to either, when boiled, making a great difference. When roasted, a chicken will be vastly improved in flavour if its own liver, chopped up with some tarragon leaves and then pounded with a good piece of butter, is placed inside the bird before it goes to the oven. The principal use of tarragon, however, is in the mixture that the French call *fines herbes*, which is used so extensively in their cooking and in dressing salads. This consists of the four herbs—tarragon, parsley, chives, and chervil—in equal parts, very finely chopped and carefully mixed together. A salad of plain lettuce without this charming addition is like a salmon mayonnaise without the mayonnaise ! The *fines herbes* should be sprinkled lightly over the salad before it is dressed, but they should not be mixed with the dressing, as their principal charm lies in their freshness, which would be lost if they were soaked in the vinegar. *Fines herbes* are excellent when mixed with mashed potato.

HORSERADISH

This is seldom used in this country save scraped or in a sauce, with beef. In Sweden a purée of apples cooked with a little white wine, into which is stirred some grated horseradish, is popular with certain meat dishes, and a mayonnaise is flavoured in the same way.

THYME

This has already been mentioned in the parsley paragraph as being one of the components of the *bouquet garni*. Apart from its further use for stuffings, there are possibilities in the use of the specially-flavoured thymes, such as Lemon Thyme, in custards and creams, the leaves being infused in the milk before the custard is made.

FENNEL

This herb was at one time used in England for a fish sauce as commonly as parsley is now, chopped blanched fennel leaves being added to a white sauce in the same way as parsley, with which it was sometimes combined. A simpler fennel sauce needs merely the addition of the chopped blanched leaves to melted butter, and this will be found to be excellent with mackerel and, according to many, also with salmon. The fennel that many of us have eaten on the Continent is Florence Fennel, which is earthed up like celery. The heads are left to soak, after they have been trimmed, in salt water for half an hour and can then be boiled or braised in the same way as celery. When cooked they may also be dressed with cheese and served *au gratin*.

SORREL

The principal uses of sorrel are as a vegetable rather than a herb, although its astringent leaves give a pleasant taste to a salad. With certain dishes of white meat, or those with which spinach goes particularly well, sorrel can be used as a purée, being cooked in the same way as spinach. Pick as young as possible, and, if necessary, strip off the stalks. Wash them in several waters, and drain well, then boil them gently in water for five minutes. A scant half-pint of water would be enough for a pound of the leaves

Pc 225

(which will be enough for two people), and it is wiser to stir the leaves with a wooden spoon as they boil, for they easily stick to the sides of the pan. After five minutes' boiling, turn the leaves into a colander, and let them drain well again. Now chop them finely on a board, and put them back into the pan in which you have mixed a spoonful of flour with the same quantity of melted butter. Then pour in about a coffee-cupful of white stock, and simmer for about an hour with the lid on the pan, stirring occasionally. If desired, one can bind this purée with a yolk of egg beaten up in a little cream.

BORAGE

This is a pretty enough herb, but I doubt if it has any serious kitchen use. Its leaves and flowers look very handsome in a white wine cup, but nowadays the stronger flavour of cucumber peel itself is preferred.

CHERVIL

This delicate little plant is, as already indicated, one of the ingredients of *fines herbes*. It goes well with chicken and with eggs, and the fine little leaves are greatly used in garnishing cold jellied dishes, meat, fish, and eggs, to which they also impart its charming but fugitive flavour. The smallest pieces of the leaves, known as *pluches* in culinary language, are used for garnishing soups.

MARJORAM

This herb has a flavour which many prefer to thyme, and is therefore often used to supplant the latter in stuffings or in the *bouquet garni*. A sprinkling over a joint of roast pork is vastly preferable to sage, which is sometimes recommended for use in this way.

SAVORY

This attractive-looking and pleasantly smelling herb, reminiscent a little of sage without its coarseness of flavour, is used in France to cook with broad beans and also with peas. We Britons are too wedded to our love of plainly-cooked green peas to like this fashion ; but those who like peas cooked *à la française* should try it. With broad beans, it is wholly to be commended, but it must be remembered that the beans should be cooked without their skins. Shell the beans and put them into boiling water and let them boil for a few minutes. Take them out and they will easily slip out of the skins. Now put them into a saucepan containing just enough water to cover them, add a few sprigs of savory, salt, of course, and cook them gently until they are tender. Drain the water off, dry the beans quickly over the fire, add a piece of butter, roll the beans in it carefully so as not to break them, and serve them. One may add a very little finely-chopped savory leaves afterwards, if the flavour is much liked, but these would have to be blanched first or they would be too strong.

BASIL

This is a herb that is sadly neglected. It is used principally in the making of turtle soup, also mock turtle soup, when its flavour is easily recognised. Its principal virtue, however, lies in its marvellous affinity for tomatoes, and I would go so far as to say that no tomato soup or sauce should be made without at any rate a touch of basil in it. It should certainly be tried in forcemeats.

ROSEMARY

I have taken this out of another section of the *Bulletin* because there is a dish in which it is used that is so good that it ought to be better known. The strong leaves of this plant are used in Italy for flavouring a ragout of veal, but in Germany they are used mainly in the following dish of hare, or, better still, leveret : For it, you want the whole of the back of the leveret, which the French call the *râble* and is really the whole of the back from the neck to the hind legs. Skin it down to the flesh and put some pieces of fat bacon over the top. Now roast this on a bed of chopped onions and carrots with a *bouquet garni* of thyme, parsley, bayleaf, and a sprig of rosemary in the middle. When it is nearly done, take off the bacon to let the back brown, and when it is done, take out the vegetables and the bouquet and pour into the pan a cupful of cream. Stir this well with the juices left in the pan, and let it boil up; add a touch of lemon juice and pour it over the leveret.

CORIANDER

Coriander, which has an orangy flavour, is used in cakes and biscuits as well as to flavour custards.

DILL

The seeds of this herb are sometimes used for flavouring vinegar, in which it is steeped for a few days before the vinegar is wanted. It has, however, lost the popularity it enjoyed two hundred or so years ago. Its leaves are used in Scandinavia in flavouring sauces for meat. It is also used largely in Germany in the pickling of cucumbers, as it was at one time in this country.

CARAWAY

I should have added Caraway, as the seeds of this herb are used in Hungary in the well known *Goulash*, a stew of meat, onions, potatoes, and paprika pepper. As this is a dish worth trying, I give it here : Cut three medium-sized onions in thin slices, and brown them in a pan in a little lard with about a pound and a half of beef cut in two-inch squares. Add a little salt, a teaspoonful of cara-way seeds in a muslin bag, one or two teaspoonfuls of paprika pepper, three or four peeled and chopped tomatoes, and half a cupful of water. Cover, and cook for an hour and a half to two hours, then add a cupful of water and seven or eight smallish peeled potatoes. Cover again, and cook for another hour, when the potatoes should be done but still whole. Then serve very hot.

CHIVES

Chives are really a very small onion, quite easy to grow and best propagated, I have found, by division. The tiny bulbs are used by some for pickling, but the real value of the plant lies in the grassy leaves which it throws up in great profusion. As it possesses a pretty mauve flower, rather like thrift, it makes a useful border plant for the kitchen or herb garden. As I have said, the leaves are one of the ingredients of *fines herbes*, but they are very good if used by themselves, finely chopped, especially with mashed potatoes, with potato salad (instead of onion), and in omelettes. Those who like a flavoured cream cheese can make an excellent one by beating up some of the chopped leaves with one, or some chopped *fines herbes*, if chives alone have too oniony a flavour.

BAY

This, of course, is not a herb, but it has been mentioned in the *bouquet garni*. The only comment I wish to make here is that, in a great many carelessly translated cookery books, the French for Bay (*laurier*) has been given as Laurel. It would hardly be pleasant to include a laurel leaf in your *bouquet garni*, so if any of my readers come across this far too common mistake they will be on their guard. Bayleaves, by the way, have an affinity in flavour with cauliflower, as will be discovered if, when next a cauliflower soup is made, a bayleaf is added or infused in the milk.

CONCLUSION

I have touched here on a number of uses for various herbs in the kitchen, and, on looking through what I have written, I can see how slight my knowledge is. In most European countries, there are recipes depending almost entirely on certain herbs for their flavour, but it would take a lifetime to make an exhaustive study of them. In Switzerland, for instance, thyme is used for flavouring a certain cheese ; in the south of France, fennel is more widely employed than elsewhere ; in Brittany, mint is added to the *bouquet garni* in a certain fish soup ; while, in America, sage, I believe, is put to more uses than could be thought possible. Perhaps after a few more years' experience in the art and practice of cooking, I may be able to return to this entrancing subject. Meanwhile, like Candide, I must " *cultiver mon jardin.*"

A CALENDAR OF
HOME-GROWN VEGETABLES

A CALENDAR OF
HOME-GROWN VEGETABLES

EVERYONE who has a kitchen garden knows what a difference the freshness of vegetables makes in cooking. To be able to gather one's own vegetables out of the garden and cook them then and there is a great privilege to the gourmet. But there are times when the size of our garden or our means or the weather conspire to rob us of this pleasure, and we should then remember that all the year round there are vegetables grown in this country which are far fresher than those imported can ever be.

To encourage our people to ask for their own home-grown vegetables, the Flowers, Plants, and Vegetables Publicity Committee has issued a Calendar of Home-Grown Vegetables, which they have kindly allowed me to reproduce here. Each month the Committee issues an interesting leaflet giving recipes for the home-grown vegetables in season, and copies of these can be had from the Secretary of the Committee at 68 Victoria Street, London, S.W.1.

HOME-GROWN VEGETABLES AND THEIR SEASONS

If you have a special liking for any particular kind of vegetable, this list will show just when it is in season and when you may expect to find it in the shops.

Artichokes
    Jerusalem . . . . September to March
    Globe . . . . June to September

Asparagus
    Outdoor . . . . April to June
    Forced . . . November to February

Beans
    Broad . . . . June to August
    Dwarf . . . . June to October
    Dwarf, Hothouse . . . March to May;
        October and November
    Runner . . . July to October

Beetroot . . . . All the year round

Broccoli
    Hearting . . . Mid-December to June
    Sprouting . . . March to May

Brussels Sprouts . . September to March

Cabbage . . . . All the year round

Cabbage, *Red* . . . October to December

Carrots
    Outdoor . . . . June to March
    Forced . . . . April to June

Cauliflower
    Outdoor . . . June to December
    Under Glass . . . May and June

Celeriac	October
Celery	August to March
Corn Salad . . .	September to November
Cucumber	All the year round
Curly Kale	November to March
Endive, *Outdoor* . .	September to November
Leeks	June to April
Lettuce	
Outdoor . . .	Late April to November
Glasshouse . . .	December and January
Under Glass . . .	March, April, November
Marrows	
Outdoor	June to November
Forced	April to June
Mint	
Outdoor	April to November
Forced	December to May
Mushrooms, *Hothouse* . .	All the year round
Mustard and Cress . . .	All the year round
Onions	September to March
Onions, *Spring* . .	February to September
Parsley	All the year round
Parsnips	August to March
Peas	Mid-June to October
Potatoes	All the year round
Potatoes, *New*	May to July

Radishes
    Outdoor . . . . April to November
    Forced . . . . February to April
Rhubarb
    Outdoor . . . Late February to June
    Forced . . . . January to April
Salsify . . . . January to May;
                       September and October

Savoys . . . . September to April

Scotch Kale . . . November to March

Seakale
    Natural . 3 weeks season in late April or May
    Forced . . . . December to April

Shallots . . . . November to January

Sorrel . September and throughout salad season

Spinach . . . . All the year round

Spring Greens . . . January to April

Swedes . . . . . September to May

Tomatoes, *Hothouse*. . . March to December

Turnips
    Outdoor . . . . . June to April
    Forced . . . . . April to June

Turnip Tops . . . . January to April

Watercress . . . . All the year round

THERE IS A BASKET OF HOME-GROWN
VEGETABLES FOR EVERY MONTH

You can buy home-grown vegetables at any time of the year. Here is a calendar showing you just what fresh British vegetables you can get month by month.

ALL THE YEAR ROUND

Beetroot	Mint	Potatoes
Cabbage	Mushrooms	Spinach
Carrots	Mustard and Cress	Turnips
Cucumber	Parsley	Watercress

JANUARY

Artichokes, Jerusalem	Lettuce	Savoys
Asparagus	Mint	Scotch Kale
Beetroot	Mushrooms	Seakale
Broccoli	Mustard and Cress	Shallots
Brussels Sprouts	Onions	Spinach
Cabbage	Parsley	Spring Greens
Carrots	Parsnips	Swedes
Celery	Potatoes	Turnips
Cucumber	Rhubarb	Turnip Tops
Curly Kale	Salsify	Watercress
Leeks		

FEBRUARY

Artichokes, Jerusalem	Mint	Salsify
Asparagus	Mushrooms	Savoys
Beetroot	Mustard and Cress	Scotch Kale
Broccoli	Onions	Seakale
Brussels Sprouts	Onions, Spring	Spinach
Cabbage	Parsley	Spring Greens
Carrots	Parsnips	Swedes
Celery	Potatoes	Turnips
Cucumber	Radishes	Turnip Tops
Curly Kale	Rhubarb	Watercress
Leeks		

MARCH

Artichokes, Jerusalem
Asparagus
Beans, Dwarf
Beetroot
Broccoli
Brussels Sprouts
Cabbage
Carrots
Celery
Cucumber
Curly Kale
Leeks

Lettuce
Onions, Spring
Onions
Mint
Mushrooms
Mustard and Cress
Parsley
Parsnips
Potatoes
Radishes
Rhubarb

Salsify
Savoys
Scotch Kale
Seakale
Spinach
Spring Greens
Swedes
Tomatoes
Turnips
Turnip Tops
Watercress

APRIL

Asparagus
Beans, Dwarf
Beetroot
Broccoli
Cabbage
Carrots
Cucumber
Leeks
Lettuce
Marrows

Mint
Mushrooms
Mustard and Cress
Onions, Spring
Parsley
Potatoes
Radishes
Rhubarb
Salsify

Savoys
Scotch Kale
Seakale
Spinach
Spring Greens
Tomatoes
Turnips
Turnip Tops
Watercress

MAY

Asparagus
Beans, Dwarf
Beetroot
Broccoli
Cabbage
Carrots
Cauliflower
Cucumber
Lettuce

Marrows
Mint
Mushrooms
Mustard and Cress
Onions, Spring
Parsley
Potatoes
Radishes

Rhubarb
Salsify
Sorrel
Spinach
Swedes
Tomatoes
Turnips
Watercress

JUNE

Artichokes, Globe
Asparagus
Beans, Broad
Beans, Dwarf
Beetroot
Broccoli
Cabbage
Carrots
Cauliflower

Cucumber
Leeks
Lettuce
Marrows
Mint
Mushrooms
Mustard and Cress
Onions, Spring
Peas

Parsley
Potatoes
Radishes
Rhubarb
Sorrel
Spinach
Tomatoes
Turnips
Watercress

JULY

Artichokes, Globe
Beans, Broad
Beans, Dwarf
Beans, Runner
Cabbage
Carrots
Cauliflower
Cucumber

Leeks
Lettuce
Marrows
Mint
Mushrooms
Mustard and Cress
Onions, Spring
Parsley

Peas
Potatoes
Radishes
Sorrel
Spinach
Tomatoes
Turnips
Watercress

AUGUST

Artichokes, Globe
Beans, Broad
Beans, Dwarf
Beans, Runner
Cabbage
Carrots
Cauliflower
Celery
Cucumber

Leeks
Lettuce
Marrows
Mint
Mushrooms
Mustard and Cress
Onions, Spring
Parsley
Parsnips

Peas
Potatoes
Radishes
Sorrel
Spinach
Tomatoes
Turnips
Watercress

SEPTEMBER

Artichokes, Jerusalem
and Globe
Beans, Dwarf
Beans, Runner
Beetroot
Brussels Sprouts
Cabbage
Carrots
Cauliflower
Celery
Corn Salad

Cucumber
Endive
Leeks
Lettuce
Marrows
Mint
Mushrooms
Mustard and Cress
Onions
Onions, Spring
Parsley

Parsnips
Peas
Potatoes
Radishes
Savoys
Sorrel
Spinach
Swedes
Tomatoes
Turnips
Watercress

OCTOBER

Artichokes, Jerusalem
Beans, Dwarf
Beans, Runner
Beetroot
Brussels Sprouts
Cabbage
Cabbage, Red
Carrots
Cauliflower
Celeriac
Celery

Corn Salad
Cucumber
Endive
Leeks
Lettuce
Marrows
Mint
Mushrooms
Mustard and Cress
Onions
Parsley

Parsnips
Peas
Potatoes
Radishes
Savoys
Spinach
Swedes
Tomatoes
Turnips
Watercress

NOVEMBER

Artichokes, Jerusalem
Asparagus
Beans, Dwarf
Beetroot
Brussels Sprouts
Cabbage
Cabbage, Red
Carrots
Cauliflower
Celery
Corn Salad

Cucumber
Curly Kale
Endive
Leeks
Lettuce
Marrows
Mint
Mushrooms
Mustard and Cress
Onions
Parsley

Parsnips
Potatoes
Radishes
Savoys
Scotch Kale
Shallots
Spinach
Swedes
Tomatoes
Turnips
Watercress

DECEMBER

Artichokes, Jerusalem
Asparagus
Beetroot
Broccoli
Brussels Sprouts
Cabbage
Cabbage, Red
Carrots
Cauliflower
Celery

Cucumber
Curly Kale
` Leeks
Lettuce
Mint
Mushrooms
Mustard and Cress
Onions
Parsley
Parsnips

Potatoes
Savoys
Scotch Kale
Seakale
Shallots
Spinach
Swedes
Tomatoes
Turnips
Watercress

THE VEGETABLE YEAR

Lastly, it may be useful to append here a list of times for sowing and planting vegetables, as a reminder. People with small gardens, like myself, will probably find the planting list more useful if they buy their plants, as seedlings usually speak for themselves when it is time to plant them out! Many who do their own gardening may like such a list in handy form, and if it is included in a cookery book I can only excuse it by saying that the vegetables are, after all, only the concern of the kitchen! As the list is mainly for the smaller garden, where not much sowing under glass, if any, is done, the times for sowing are for open sowing.

	Sow in open	Plant out
Artichoke		
Globe . .	March and April	April
Jerusalem . .		February and March
Asparagus . .		March and April
Beans		
Broad . .	November to April	
Dwarf . .	Late April to July	
Runner . .	May and June	
Beetroot . .	April to July	
Broccoli . .	March to May	May to July
Brussels Sprouts .	March and April	May and June
Cabbage .	March to May	May to July
	August	September to February
Carrot . .	March to August	
Cauliflower . .	March to May	April to July
	August and	
	September	February and March
Celeriac . .	April	May and June
Celery . . .	April	May and June
Cucumber		
Ridge . .	May	May and June

242

	Sow in open	Plant out
Endive . .	April to August	
Kale . . .	March to May	June and July
Leek . .	February and March	April to July
Lettuce .	March to September	
Maize		
Sweet Corn .	April and May	May
Onion . .	March to July	February and March
	August	February
Parsley .	March to July	
Parsnip .	February and March	
Pea		
Round .	November to July	
Wrinkled .	March to July	
Potato .	January to April	
	July	
Radish .	March to September	
Salsify .	April and May	
Savoy . .	March to May	May to July
Seakale .	March and April	March
Shallot . .		February or earlier
Spinach		
Summer .	February to August	
Winter .	July to September	
Perpetual .	April to July	
New Zealand .	May	
Turnip .	April to August	
Vegetable Marrow	May	May and June

CLASSIFIED INDEX

CLASSIFIED INDEX

SOUPS

EGGS

EGGS (*continued*)

FISH

FISH (*continued*)

MEAT, POULTRY AND GAME

VEGETABLES (*continued*)

HERBS

HERBS (*continued*)

SWEETS

SAVOURY DISHES

MISCELLANEOUS

If you have enjoyed this Persephone book why not telephone or write to us for a free copy of the *Persephone Catalogue* and the current *Persephone Biannually*? All Persephone books ordered from us cost £12 or three for £30 plus £2 postage per book.

PERSEPHONE BOOKS LTD
59 Lamb's Conduit Street
London WC1N 3NB

Telephone: 020 7242 9292
sales@persephonebooks.co.uk
www.persephonebooks.co.uk